I0012443

# Table of Contents

# Introduction

Software Asset Management (S.A.M) is the practice of effectively managing an organization's software assets throughout their lifecycle, from procurement to disposal. S.A.M helps organizations to optimize their software licenses, reduce costs, and mitigate legal and security risks associated with software usage.

By implementing S.A.M, organizations can ensure that they are using the right software products for their needs, that they are using them efficiently, and that they are in compliance with relevant licensing agreements. S.A.M involves inventorying software assets, tracking license compliance, optimizing license usage, and aligning software purchasing with business needs.

Effective S.A.M requires cross-functional collaboration between IT, procurement, legal, and other stakeholders, and the use of specialized S.A.M tools and processes. By proactively managing their software assets, organizations can reduce costs, mitigate risks, and make informed decisions about future software purchases. S.A.M is an essential practice for any organization that uses software, and it should be an integral part of the overall IT and business strategy.

**Effective S.A.M can help organizations in several ways, such as:**

1. **Cost Reduction:** By optimizing software usage and avoiding over-licensing or under-licensing, organizations can reduce their software costs.
2. **Legal Compliance:** S.A.M helps organizations comply with licensing agreements and avoid legal and financial risks associated with non-compliance.
3. **Security:** S.A.M ensures that software products are up-to-date, secure, and free of vulnerabilities, thereby reducing security risks.
4. **Procurement Efficiency:** S.A.M helps organizations align software purchasing with business needs, negotiate better contracts with vendors, and optimize license usage.
5. **IT Asset Management:** S.A.M is an integral part of IT Asset Management (ITAM) that helps organizations manage their hardware and software assets effectively.

S.A.M is a complex process that involves several stages and requires collaboration between different departments within an organization. Some of the key stages in the S.A.M process include:

6. **Software Inventory:** Organizations must identify and catalog all software products in use, including details such as version, edition, and number of licenses.
7. **License Management:** S.A.M requires organizations to track license entitlements,

monitor usage, and ensure compliance with licensing agreements.

8. **Software Usage Monitoring:** Organizations must monitor software usage to identify over-licensing and under-licensing.

9. **Optimization:** S.A.M helps organizations optimize their software usage, which may include consolidating licenses, purchasing additional licenses, or adjusting usage patterns.

10. **Vendor Management:** S.A.M requires organizations to manage relationships with software vendors, negotiate contracts, and maintain compliance with licensing agreements.

11. **Disposal:** S.A.M requires organizations to properly dispose of unused or obsolete software products.

Effective S.A.M also requires the use of specialized S.A.M tools and processes, such as license management software, automated inventory tools, and contract management software.

S.A.M has become increasingly important in recent years due to the rise of cloud-based software, which has complicated software licensing and asset management. Cloud-based software is often licensed on a subscription basis, and organizations may use multiple cloud services from various vendors, making it difficult to keep track of license entitlements, usage, and costs.

Furthermore, the COVID-19 pandemic has accelerated the adoption of remote work, making software asset management even more critical. Remote workers may use a variety of devices and applications, making it challenging to ensure license compliance, monitor usage, and maintain security.

Effective S.A.M can help organizations overcome these challenges and ensure that they are using software products efficiently, cost-effectively, and in compliance with licensing agreements.

S.A.M is a complex process that requires cross-functional collaboration and specialized tools and processes, but the benefits to an organization are significant.

By adopting S.A.M best practices, organizations can ensure that they are using software products in the most efficient and cost-effective way possible.

In conclusion, S.A.M is a critical practice for any organization that uses software. It involves managing software assets throughout their lifecycle, optimizing license usage, and ensuring compliance with licensing agreements. Effective S.A.M can help organizations reduce costs, mitigate risks, and make informed decisions about future software purchases. With the increasing complexity of software licensing and the rise of cloud-based software and remote work, S.A.M has become more important than ever.

## Software License Compliance

Software license compliance is a critical aspect of software asset management (S.A.M) that ensures an organization is using software products in accordance with the terms and conditions of the license agreement. License compliance involves monitoring and verifying software usage against license entitlements and identifying instances of over-licensing or under-licensing.

Over-licensing occurs when an organization has more licenses than it needs to support its software usage, resulting in unnecessary costs. Under-licensing occurs when an organization uses more software products than it has licenses for, which can result in legal and financial risks.

To ensure license compliance, organizations must track license entitlements, monitor usage, and reconcile usage against entitlements. This requires implementing a license management process that includes regular monitoring of software usage, license utilization analysis, and license reconciliation.

S.A.M tools can help organizations automate the license compliance process by providing real-time visibility into license usage and entitlements. S.A.M tools can also help organizations identify opportunities for license optimization, such as license consolidation or license pooling.

Effective license compliance also requires cross-functional collaboration between IT, procurement, and legal departments to ensure that licensing agreements are properly negotiated, tracked, and enforced. By ensuring license compliance, organizations can reduce costs, mitigate legal and financial risks, and make informed decisions about future software purchases.

Software license compliance is also critical for maintaining software security. When software is not in compliance with licensing agreements, it may not receive critical security updates or patches, leaving it vulnerable to security threats.

Non-compliance with licensing agreements can also result in legal penalties and damage to an organization's reputation. Vendors may audit an organization's software usage to ensure compliance with licensing agreements, and non-compliance can result in fines, penalties, or legal action.

To ensure license compliance, organizations must maintain accurate records of their software assets, licenses, and usage. This requires proper documentation of software entitlements, deployment, and usage. Organizations must also ensure that their license usage is aligned with their business needs, and that they are not paying for licenses they don't need.

To achieve software license compliance, organizations should follow some best practices, such as:

1. **Establish a License Management Process:** Organizations should establish a license management process that includes regular monitoring of software usage, license utilization analysis, and license reconciliation.
2. **Centralize License Management:** Organizations should centralize license management to ensure consistency and reduce the risk of non-compliance.
3. **Automate License Management:** S.A.M tools can help automate license management and provide real-time visibility into license usage and entitlements.
4. **Train Staff on License Compliance:** Organizations should train staff on license compliance to ensure they are aware of licensing agreements and their responsibilities.
5. **Maintain Accurate Records:** Organizations should maintain accurate records of software entitlements, deployment, and usage to ensure compliance with licensing agreements.
6. **Conduct Regular Audits:** Organizations should conduct regular audits of their software usage to ensure compliance with licensing agreements and identify opportunities for license optimization.
7. **Negotiate Favorable Licensing Agreements:** Organizations should negotiate favorable licensing agreements that align with their

business needs and ensure compliance with licensing agreements.

Additionally, S.A.M can also help organizations with software license compliance by providing insight into the types of licenses being used, how often they are being used, and how they can be optimized. S.A.M tools can generate detailed reports that show which licenses are being used the most and which licenses are being underutilized or not used at all. This information can be used to optimize license usage and ensure compliance with licensing agreements.

S.A.M can also help organizations to manage the risks associated with software license compliance. For example, organizations can use S.A.M to ensure that all software is properly licensed, that software licenses are renewed on time, and that they are in compliance with software license agreements.

S.A.M also helps organizations with vendor management, ensuring that they are working with reputable vendors and that they are negotiating favorable licensing agreements. S.A.M can help organizations to identify licensing options that are more cost-effective, such as using open-source software, or moving to a subscription-based licensing model.

In conclusion, software license compliance is a critical aspect of S.A.M that ensures an organization is using software products in accordance with the terms and conditions of the license agreement. It requires regular monitoring of software usage, license utilization analysis, and license reconciliation. S.A.M tools can help automate the license compliance process and provide real-time visibility into license usage and entitlements. By ensuring license compliance, organizations can reduce costs, mitigate legal and financial risks, and maintain software security.

## Software License Reconciliation

Software License Reconciliation is a process of verifying the number of software licenses owned by an organization, comparing it to the number of licenses in use, and identifying any discrepancies. The purpose of license reconciliation is to ensure that an organization is not over- or under-licensed, which can lead to unnecessary costs or compliance issues.

The license reconciliation process typically involves the following steps:

1. **Collecting software license information:** Gathering information on all software licenses owned by the organization, including the type of license, the number of licenses, the terms and conditions of the license agreement, and the license expiration date.
2. **Collecting software usage information:** Gathering information on the number of licenses in use, including the number of licenses

deployed, the number of licenses being used, and the number of licenses that are not being used.

3. **Comparing license information and usage information:** Comparing the license information and usage information to identify any discrepancies or gaps.

4. **Identifying discrepancies and gaps:** Identifying discrepancies and gaps between the license information and usage information, and taking steps to resolve any issues.

5. **Adjusting license inventory:** Adjusting the license inventory to reflect the actual number of licenses needed by the organization.

6. **Updating license agreements:** Updating license agreements to ensure that they accurately reflect the number of licenses needed by the organization.

7. **Developing a license compliance plan:** Developing a license compliance plan to ensure that the organization remains compliant with licensing agreements and regulations.

By conducting license reconciliation, organizations can ensure that they are using their software assets efficiently and effectively, while avoiding unnecessary costs or compliance issues. S.A.M tools can be used to automate and streamline the license reconciliation process, allowing organizations to identify discrepancies and gaps more quickly and accurately.

Software License Reconciliation also helps organizations to identify areas for software license optimization. By analyzing the license information and usage information, organizations can determine which licenses are being underutilized and which licenses are being overutilized. This information can be used to optimize software licensing, reduce software costs, and ensure compliance with license agreements.

The license reconciliation process is an ongoing process and should be conducted regularly to ensure that the organization's software inventory is accurate and up-to-date. This can help to reduce the risk of non-compliance and ensure that the organization is using its software assets effectively and efficiently.

Software License Reconciliation can also be a complex and time-consuming process, especially for large organizations with a large number of software applications and licenses. S.A.M tools can help to automate and streamline the license reconciliation process, making it faster, more accurate, and less prone to human error.

License reconciliation can also help organizations to avoid the risks associated with software audits and to manage their relationships with software vendors more effectively. By conducting regular license reconciliations, organizations can ensure that they are maintaining accurate and up-to-date software inventories and are using their software assets in compliance with licensing agreements. This can help to reduce the risk of non-compliance and minimize the financial impact of software audits.

In addition, license reconciliation can help organizations to negotiate better software licensing agreements with vendors. By having a detailed and accurate understanding of their software usage and license requirements, organizations can better negotiate volume licensing agreements and other contractual terms with vendors. This can help to reduce software costs and improve the overall value of software assets.

Software License Reconciliation can also help organizations to manage their software assets in the cloud. With the rise of cloud computing, software licensing has become more complex, and it can be challenging to track software usage across multiple cloud platforms and vendors. License reconciliation can help organizations to maintain an accurate and up-to-date inventory of cloud-based software assets, monitor usage, and manage licensing costs.

In addition, license reconciliation can help organizations to prepare for mergers, acquisitions, and divestitures. During these types of corporate events, it is essential to have an accurate and up-to-date understanding of an organization's software assets and licensing agreements. By conducting regular license reconciliations, organizations can ensure that they are well-prepared for corporate events and that their software assets are effectively managed throughout the process.

Software License Reconciliation is an essential process for any organization that relies on software to support its operations. By managing software licensing effectively and efficiently, organizations can reduce software costs, optimize the use of their software assets, and ensure compliance with licensing agreements and regulations. S.A.M tools can help to automate and streamline the license reconciliation process, making it faster, more accurate, and more effective.

Overall, Software License Reconciliation is a critical process for organizations that rely on software to support their operations. By managing software licensing effectively and efficiently, organizations can reduce software costs, minimize the risk of non-compliance, and optimize the use of their software assets. S.A.M tools can help to streamline and automate the license reconciliation process, making it faster, more accurate, and more effective.

## Software License Optimization

Software license optimization is the process of optimizing software licenses to reduce costs and ensure compliance with license agreements. By optimizing licenses, organizations can reduce the number of licenses they need to purchase and ensure that they are using the licenses they have in the most cost-effective way possible.

Here are some ways that S.A.M (Software Asset Management) can help with software license optimization:

1. **License Tracking:** S.A.M tools can track all software licenses and ensure that an organization has the appropriate number of licenses for their software usage.
2. **License Reconciliation:** S.A.M can help reconcile software license usage with licenses to ensure compliance and avoid the overuse of licenses.
3. **License Metrics:** S.A.M can help understand software license metrics and ensure that licenses are assigned correctly, such as user-based or device-based licenses.
4. **Data Analysis:** S.A.M can provide data analysis tools to help identify license usage patterns and areas where licenses can be optimized.
5. **License Optimization:** S.A.M can help optimize software licenses by identifying unused or underutilized licenses and consolidating licenses where possible.
6. **Compliance Reporting:** S.A.M can generate compliance reports that show an organization's compliance status and identify any areas where it is not in compliance. This can help

organizations avoid non-compliance and costly fines associated with non-compliance.

By using S.A.M to manage software licenses and optimize license usage, organizations can reduce costs and ensure compliance with license agreements. This can result in significant cost savings over time and help organizations better manage their overall software investments.

## List Software License Types

Here are some common software license types:

1. **Perpetual license:** A license that allows you to use the software indefinitely without additional payments.
2. **Subscription license:** A license that grants you the right to use the software for a specific period of time, typically one year.
3. **Concurrent license**: A license that allows a specific number of users to use the software at the same time.
4. **Node-locked license:** A license that is tied to a specific machine or hardware device.
5. **Server-based license:** A license that allows the software to be installed on a server and accessed by multiple users.
6. **Core-based license:** A license that is based on the number of CPU cores in the machine on which the software is installed.

7. **User-based license:** A license that is based on the number of users who will be using the software.
8. **Device-based license:** A license that is based on the number of devices that will be using the software.
9. **Open source license:** A license that allows you to use, modify, and distribute the software freely, subject to certain conditions.
10. **Commercial license:** A license that grants you the right to use the software for commercial purposes, typically for a fee.

## Software Vendor Management

Software vendor management is a critical aspect of software asset management (S.A.M) that involves managing relationships with software vendors, negotiating contracts, and maintaining compliance with licensing agreements. Software vendors are important partners for organizations that use software, and effective vendor management can help organizations to optimize their software usage, reduce costs, and mitigate legal and financial risks.

Vendor management involves several stages, including:

1. **Vendor Selection:** Organizations must identify and select software vendors that align with their

business needs and provide high-quality products and services.

2. **Contract Negotiation:** Organizations must negotiate contracts that provide favorable terms and conditions, including licensing terms, pricing, support, and maintenance.

3. **Contract Management:** Organizations must manage the contract throughout its lifecycle, including monitoring compliance with licensing agreements, renewing contracts, and enforcing terms and conditions.

4. **Vendor Performance Management:** Organizations must evaluate vendor performance and hold vendors accountable for meeting performance standards.

Effective vendor management requires cross-functional collaboration between IT, procurement, and legal departments. Organizations must also establish vendor management policies and procedures that ensure consistency and compliance with relevant laws and regulations.

S.A.M tools can help organizations manage vendor relationships by providing real-time visibility into license usage, vendor performance, and compliance with licensing agreements. S.A.M tools can also help organizations negotiate better contracts with vendors, optimize license usage, and reduce costs.

Effective software vendor management also involves managing vendor risk. Organizations must ensure that their software vendors are reputable, comply with relevant laws and regulations, and have adequate security measures in place to protect software and data. Organizations must also monitor vendor performance to ensure that vendors meet performance standards and are delivering quality products and services.

Vendor management also involves ensuring that software vendors comply with licensing agreements. Organizations must monitor software usage and license entitlements to ensure compliance with licensing agreements, negotiate favorable licensing terms, and ensure that vendors are held accountable for meeting licensing obligations.

In addition, vendor management involves identifying opportunities for cost optimization, such as consolidating licenses, purchasing additional licenses, or adjusting usage patterns. S.A.M tools can help organizations identify these opportunities and negotiate more favorable pricing and licensing terms with vendors.

Some best practices for software vendor management include:

1. **Vendor Selection:** Organizations should select software vendors that align with their business

needs, have a good reputation, and provide high-quality products and services.

2. **Contract Negotiation:** Organizations should negotiate contracts that provide favorable terms and conditions, including licensing terms, pricing, support, and maintenance.

3. **Contract Management:** Organizations should manage the contract throughout its lifecycle, including monitoring compliance with licensing agreements, renewing contracts, and enforcing terms and conditions.

4. **Vendor Performance Management:** Organizations should evaluate vendor performance regularly and hold vendors accountable for meeting performance standards.

5. **Vendor Risk Management:** Organizations should manage vendor risk by ensuring that vendors comply with relevant laws and regulations, have adequate security measures in place, and meet performance standards.

6. **Regular Audits:** Organizations should conduct regular audits of vendor performance, contract compliance, and software usage to identify opportunities for optimization and cost reduction.

7. **S.A.M Tools:** Organizations should use S.A.M tools to automate vendor management tasks,

provide real-time visibility into license usage, and optimize license usage.

Effective software vendor management is essential for optimizing software usage, reducing costs, and mitigating legal, financial, and security risks. By following these best practices and using S.A.M tools, organizations can manage their vendor relationships more effectively, negotiate better contracts, and maintain compliance with licensing agreements.

In addition, effective software vendor management also involves establishing clear communication channels with vendors. Organizations must ensure that there is clear communication between IT, procurement, and legal departments and the vendor to ensure that issues are resolved quickly and effectively. Establishing open communication channels can help to reduce misunderstandings, facilitate problem resolution, and promote a positive relationship between the organization and the vendor.

Organizations must also ensure that they have proper documentation of their vendor relationships, including contracts, licensing agreements, and performance metrics. Proper documentation is critical for managing vendor relationships effectively and for ensuring compliance with relevant laws and regulations.

Another best practice for software vendor management is to conduct regular vendor performance evaluations. Organizations should establish key performance indicators (KPIs) for vendor performance, such as on-time delivery, responsiveness to support requests, and meeting service level agreements (SLAs). These KPIs should be regularly evaluated and reported to ensure that vendors are meeting performance standards.

Finally, effective software vendor management involves ongoing optimization of software usage and license management. Organizations should regularly monitor software usage and license entitlements to ensure that they are aligned with business needs and identify opportunities for license optimization. S.A.M tools can help organizations automate license management, monitor license usage, and identify opportunities for optimization.

In conclusion, effective software vendor management is an essential aspect of S.A.M that involves managing relationships with software vendors, negotiating contracts, and maintaining compliance with licensing agreements. Effective vendor management requires clear communication channels, proper documentation, regular vendor performance evaluations, and ongoing optimization of software usage and license management. By following these best practices, organizations can optimize their software usage, reduce costs, and mitigate legal, financial, and security risks.

## Software Inventory

Software inventory is a critical aspect of software asset management (S.A.M) that involves identifying and cataloging all software products in use, including details such as version, edition, and number of licenses. Software inventory provides organizations with a complete view of their software assets, enabling them to manage and optimize software usage, reduce costs, and mitigate legal and security risks.

The software inventory process involves several stages, including:

1. **Discovery:** Organizations must identify all devices and systems within their network that may be running software, including desktops, laptops, servers, and mobile devices.
2. **Inventory Collection:** Once devices and systems have been identified, organizations must collect an inventory of all software products installed on these devices and systems. This inventory should include details such as version, edition, and number of licenses.
3. **Inventory Management:** Organizations must manage the software inventory, ensuring that it is up to date, accurate, and comprehensive.
4. **Inventory Optimization:** Once the inventory has been collected and managed, organizations must optimize software usage, identify

opportunities for license consolidation, and ensure compliance with licensing agreements.

S.A.M tools can help automate the software inventory process, making it easier for organizations to identify all devices and systems on their network and collect an inventory of all software products installed on these devices and systems. S.A.M tools can also help organizations optimize software usage, identify license optimization opportunities, and ensure compliance with licensing agreements.

Effective software inventory requires regular monitoring and updating of the inventory to ensure that it is up to date and comprehensive. This requires establishing policies and procedures for managing the inventory, ensuring that it is accurate, and monitoring software usage to identify opportunities for optimization.

In addition, effective software inventory management also involves identifying and tracking software dependencies. Software products often depend on other software products to function properly, and identifying these dependencies is critical for managing software assets effectively. By understanding software dependencies, organizations can optimize their software usage, reduce costs, and mitigate security risks.

Another best practice for software inventory management is to establish a process for managing software updates and patches. Organizations must ensure that their software inventory is up to date and that all software products have the latest updates and patches to maintain software security and functionality.

Software inventory management also involves managing legacy software products. Legacy software products can present security risks, and organizations must ensure that they are properly managed and updated to maintain software security. Legacy software products may also be subject to licensing agreements, and organizations must ensure that they are in compliance with these agreements.

Finally, software inventory management involves ongoing optimization of software usage and license management. Organizations should regularly monitor software usage and license entitlements to ensure that they are aligned with business needs and identify opportunities for license optimization. S.A.M tools can help organizations automate license management, monitor license usage, and identify opportunities for optimization.

To achieve effective software inventory management, organizations should follow some best practices, such as:

1. **Establish a Software Inventory Process:** Organizations should establish a software inventory process that includes regular monitoring of software usage, inventory collection, management, and optimization.

2. **Automate Software Inventory:** S.A.M tools can help automate the software inventory process, making it easier for organizations to manage and optimize software usage.

3. **Track Software Dependencies:** Organizations should track software dependencies to ensure that all software products are functioning properly and mitigate security risks.

4. **Manage Legacy Software Products:** Organizations should manage legacy software products to ensure that they are properly updated and secured.

5. **Manage Software Updates and Patches:** Organizations should ensure that all software products have the latest updates and patches to maintain software security and functionality.

6. **Regular Audits:** Organizations should conduct regular audits of their software inventory to ensure that it is up to date and comprehensive.

7. **S.A.M Tools:** Organizations should use S.A.M tools to automate inventory management tasks, provide real-time visibility into license usage, and optimize license usage.

S.A.M tools can provide organizations with real-time visibility into their software inventory, making it easier to identify license compliance issues, software usage patterns, and opportunities for cost optimization. S.A.M tools can also help organizations automate inventory management tasks, including inventory collection, management, and optimization.

Effective software inventory management can also help organizations to manage their software assets more efficiently. By maintaining an accurate inventory of software assets, organizations can identify opportunities for license optimization, such as consolidating licenses or purchasing additional licenses. This can help organizations reduce costs and optimize software usage.

In addition, software inventory management can help organizations maintain software security. By ensuring that all software products are up to date and have the latest patches and updates, organizations can mitigate security risks and protect their software and data.

In conclusion, effective software inventory management is a critical aspect of S.A.M that involves identifying and cataloging all software products in use, including details such as version, edition, and number of licenses. S.A.M tools can help automate inventory management tasks, provide real-time visibility into license usage, and optimize license usage. By following best practices for software inventory management, organizations can optimize software usage, reduce costs, and mitigate legal, financial, and security risks.

## S.A.M tools

There are several software asset management (S.A.M) tools available in the market, each with its own unique set of features and capabilities. Here are some popular S.A.M tools:

1. **Flexera FlexNet Manager Suite:** Provides visibility into software usage and license compliance across the entire organization.
2. **Snow License Manager:** Offers a complete view of software inventory, usage, and license entitlements, and provides recommendations for license optimization.
3. **Ivanti IT Asset Management Suite:** Enables organizations to manage their software assets and optimize software usage.
4. **BMC Helix Discovery:** Provides automated discovery and mapping of all hardware and software assets within an organization.
5. **ServiceNow Software Asset Management:** Offers a centralized view of software inventory and usage, and provides recommendations for license optimization.
6. **Microsoft Endpoint Manager:** Provides centralized management of devices and applications, including software inventory and usage.

7. **Symantec Asset Management Suite:** Enables organizations to manage their software and hardware assets and optimize software usage.
8. **ManageEngine AssetExplorer:** Provides a complete view of hardware and software assets and offers license optimization capabilities.
9. **LANDESK IT Asset Management Suite:** Offers a comprehensive solution for managing software and hardware assets, optimizing license usage, and ensuring license compliance.
10. **Freshservice:** Helps manage software inventory and licenses, provides real-time visibility into license usage, and automates license compliance.

Microsoft and Software Asset Management Tools

Microsoft provides a number of tools and resources to support software asset management (SAM). These tools and resources include:

1. **Microsoft License Advisor:** This online tool helps organizations to assess their software needs and select the appropriate licenses for their environment.
2. **Microsoft License Verification:** This tool enables organizations to verify their license compliance and identify potential compliance risks.
3. **Volume Licensing Service Center (VLSC):** The VLSC is a centralized portal for managing

volume licensing agreements, downloading software, and tracking license usage.

4. **Microsoft Software Inventory Analyzer (MSIA):** MSIA is a free tool that enables organizations to scan their network and create an inventory of installed Microsoft software.

5. **System Center Configuration Manager:** This tool provides a centralized platform for managing software deployment, updates, and compliance.

SharePoint and Software Asset Management Tool

SharePoint is a collaboration platform from Microsoft that allows organizations to create and manage content, documents, and workflows in a secure and centralized manner. SharePoint can be used to support a range of business functions, including software asset management (SAM).

Using SharePoint, organizations can create centralized repositories for software-related information, such as software license agreements, purchase orders, and software usage data. SharePoint can also be used to manage workflows related to software procurement, license compliance, and software audits.

Some ways that SharePoint can be used to support software asset management include:

1. **Document management:** SharePoint can be used to store and manage software license

agreements, purchase orders, and other documents related to software procurement and management.

2. **Workflow management:** SharePoint can be used to create workflows for software procurement and license compliance, including the approval and tracking of software purchases and the tracking of software usage and license compliance.

3. **Reporting and analytics:** SharePoint can be used to generate reports and analytics on software usage and license compliance, enabling organizations to identify opportunities for optimization and cost reduction.

4. **Collaboration and communication:** SharePoint can be used to support collaboration and communication between different teams and stakeholders involved in software asset management, including IT, procurement, and legal.

Overall, using SharePoint for software asset management can help organizations to improve their management of software assets, reduce risks related to license compliance, and optimize software spending.

PowerBI and Software Asset Management Tool
Power BI is a business analytics service from Microsoft that enables organizations to analyze data and share

insights through interactive visualizations and reports. Power BI can be used to support software asset management (SAM) by providing data analysis capabilities that can help organizations to track and manage software assets.

Some ways that Power BI can be used to support SAM include:

1. **License compliance:** Power BI can be used to create reports that provide insights into software usage, license compliance, and potential compliance risks.
2. **Software optimization:** Power BI can be used to generate reports that help identify opportunities for software optimization, such as identifying underutilized licenses and duplicate software.
3. **Cost reduction:** Power BI can be used to track software spend, identify cost reduction opportunities, and monitor the effectiveness of cost reduction initiatives.
4. **Vendor management:** Power BI can be used to track and manage vendor performance, identify potential issues, and track key metrics related to vendor management.

Overall, Power BI can be a valuable tool for organizations seeking to improve their management of software assets. By providing real-time data analysis capabilities and insights, Power BI can help organizations to identify risks and opportunities related to software asset management, leading to more effective decision-making and better outcomes.

It's important to note that each organization has unique needs and requirements, and S.A.M tools should be selected based on those specific needs.

When selecting a S.A.M tool, it's important to consider factors such as the size of the organization, the complexity of the software environment, the number of licenses and vendors, the degree of automation required, and the level of support and services provided by the vendor.

Additionally, some S.A.M tools are designed for specific software vendors, such as Microsoft or Oracle, and may provide more extensive capabilities for managing licenses and optimizing software usage for those vendors.

S.A.M tools can be installed on-premises or offered as a cloud-based service. Cloud-based S.A.M tools are becoming increasingly popular due to their ease of deployment, lower upfront costs, and scalability. However, organizations should ensure that they have adequate security measures in place when using cloud-based S.A.M tools to protect their software and data.

S.A.M tools can also help organizations to monitor software usage and identify opportunities for license optimization. By analyzing usage patterns, S.A.M tools can help identify underutilized licenses, provide recommendations for license consolidation, and identify opportunities for purchasing additional licenses.

S.A.M tools can also help organizations to manage license renewals and contract negotiations. By providing real-time visibility into license usage, S.A.M tools can help organizations negotiate more favorable licensing terms and avoid unnecessary license purchases.

In addition, S.A.M tools can help organizations to maintain compliance with licensing agreements. By providing real-time visibility into license usage, S.A.M tools can help identify compliance issues and ensure that organizations are in compliance with licensing agreements.

Finally, S.A.M tools can help organizations to maintain software security. By providing real-time visibility into software inventory and usage, S.A.M tools can help organizations identify security risks and take appropriate action to protect their software and data.

In addition to the benefits mentioned earlier, S.A.M tools can help organizations to achieve several other benefits, including:

1. **Improved Decision Making:** S.A.M tools provide real-time visibility into software inventory and usage, enabling organizations to make more

informed decisions about software usage, license management, and procurement.

2. **Cost Savings:** S.A.M tools can help organizations to optimize software usage, reduce costs, and avoid unnecessary license purchases.
3. **Reduced Legal and Financial Risks:** S.A.M tools can help organizations maintain compliance with licensing agreements and reduce legal and financial risks associated with non-compliance.
4. **Increased Efficiency:** S.A.M tools can help automate inventory management tasks, providing a more efficient way of managing software assets.
5. **Enhanced Security:** S.A.M tools can help organizations identify security risks and take appropriate action to protect their software and data.
6. **Better Collaboration:** S.A.M tools provide a centralized platform for managing software assets, enabling collaboration between IT, procurement, and legal departments.

In conclusion, S.A.M tools are an essential aspect of software asset management that can help organizations optimize their software usage, reduce costs, and mitigate legal, financial, and security risks. S.A.M tools provide real-time visibility into software inventory and usage, automate inventory management tasks, and identify opportunities for license optimization. By following best practices for

S.A.M and using S.A.M tools, organizations can effectively manage their software assets, make informed decisions, and collaborate more effectively between departments.

## Software Lifecycle

Software lifecycle is the process of managing software from its initial conception to its retirement. It includes several stages that are designed to ensure that software is developed, deployed, and managed in a controlled and structured manner. The stages of software lifecycle typically include:

1. **Planning:** In this stage, the scope and objectives of the software project are defined, and a plan is developed for how the software will be developed, tested, and deployed.
2. **Development:** In this stage, the software is designed, developed, and tested. The development process typically includes coding, debugging, and testing.
3. **Testing:** In this stage, the software is tested to ensure that it is free from bugs and meets the required specifications. Testing may include manual testing, automated testing, and user acceptance testing.
4. **Deployment:** In this stage, the software is deployed to production environments. This stage includes installation, configuration, and training.

5. **Maintenance:** In this stage, the software is maintained and updated to ensure that it continues to meet the needs of users. Maintenance may include bug fixes, security updates, and feature enhancements.
6. **Retirement:** In this stage, the software is retired and removed from production environments. This may include archiving data, migrating to new software, or decommissioning hardware.

Effective software lifecycle management is critical for managing software assets and ensuring that they are developed, deployed, and managed in a controlled and structured manner. By following best practices for software lifecycle management, organizations can optimize software usage, reduce costs, and mitigate legal, financial, and security risks.

Effective software lifecycle management requires the use of software development methodologies that provide a structured approach to software development, such as Waterfall, Agile, and DevOps.

Waterfall is a sequential approach to software development that involves completing one stage of the software lifecycle before moving on to the next stage. Agile is an iterative approach that involves developing software in short iterations, with regular feedback from users and stakeholders. DevOps is a methodology that integrates development and operations to improve the speed and quality of software delivery.

In addition to using software development methodologies, effective software lifecycle management also requires effective project management and collaboration between stakeholders. This involves establishing clear communication channels, setting clear goals and objectives, and managing project timelines and budgets.

S.A.M is an essential aspect of software lifecycle management that involves managing software assets from acquisition to retirement. Effective S.A.M requires a comprehensive understanding of software licensing agreements and an accurate inventory of software assets.

Effective software lifecycle management also requires ongoing monitoring of software usage and license compliance. This involves regularly monitoring software usage patterns and license entitlements to ensure that they are aligned with business needs and identify opportunities for license optimization.

Effective software lifecycle management can provide several benefits to organizations, including:

1. **Improved Software Quality:** Effective software lifecycle management can help ensure that software is developed and deployed to meet the required specifications and is free from bugs and errors.

2. **Reduced Costs:** Effective software lifecycle management can help reduce costs by optimizing software usage, avoiding unnecessary license purchases, and minimizing the time and resources required for software development and maintenance.

3. **Increased Efficiency:** Effective software lifecycle management can help improve efficiency by streamlining the software development process and enabling collaboration between stakeholders.

4. **Enhanced Security:** Effective software lifecycle management can help enhance software security by ensuring that software is up to date and free from security vulnerabilities.

5. **Improved Compliance:** Effective software lifecycle management can help ensure that organizations are in compliance with software licensing agreements and other legal requirements.

6. **Improved Decision Making:** Effective software lifecycle management can provide organizations with the information they need to make informed decisions about software development, deployment, and management.

To achieve effective software lifecycle management, organizations should follow some best practices, such as:

1. **Establish a Software Development Process:** Organizations should establish a software development process that includes clear objectives, requirements, and specifications, and a plan for how the software will be developed, tested, and deployed.
2. **Use Agile or DevOps Methodologies:** Agile and DevOps methodologies are designed to provide a structured approach to software development, enabling faster delivery and better quality.
3. **Use Automated Testing:** Automated testing can help ensure that software is free from bugs and meets the required specifications.
4. **Regular Maintenance and Updates:** Regular maintenance and updates can help ensure that software is up to date and free from security vulnerabilities.
5. **Effective Collaboration:** Effective collaboration between stakeholders, including IT, procurement, and legal departments, can help ensure that software is developed, deployed, and managed in a controlled and structured manner.
6. **Use S.A.M Tools:** S.A.M tools can help organizations monitor software usage and license compliance, optimize license usage, and reduce costs.

7. **Ongoing Monitoring:** Ongoing monitoring of software usage and license compliance can help ensure that software is being used in a way that aligns with business needs and is compliant with licensing agreements.

In conclusion, effective software lifecycle management is critical for managing software assets and ensuring that they are developed, deployed, and managed in a controlled and structured manner. By following best practices for software lifecycle management, organizations can optimize software usage, reduce costs, and mitigate legal, financial, and security risks. S.A.M tools can help automate inventory management tasks, provide real-time visibility into license usage, and optimize license usage. By combining best practices for software lifecycle management with S.A.M tools, organizations can effectively manage their software assets and achieve the benefits of effective software lifecycle management.

## Software Asset Management Methodology

**Planning:** Planning is a critical phase in the Software Asset Management (SAM) process, where organizations establish the goals, objectives, and policies for their SAM program. During this phase, the organization should identify their business and technical requirements, such as the software license types and models they need. They should also define the scope of their SAM program, such as the software inventory and the metrics they will use to measure success.

Another critical part of the planning phase is the selection of SAM tools. The organization should identify the SAM tools that meet their requirements, and evaluate the cost and benefit of each tool. They should also determine the resources needed to implement and operate the SAM tools, such as hardware, software, and personnel. Once the organization has identified the SAM tools, they should develop a plan to integrate the tools into their IT infrastructure and train the users.

**Identification:** Software asset identification involves creating an inventory of all software assets owned by an organization, including licenses, versions, and usage information. This process typically involves conducting an audit of all software installations, as well as an assessment of the company's software contracts, licenses, and entitlements. The goal is to identify all software assets, regardless of their location or installation, in order to establish a baseline for the organization's SAM program. Once this inventory is established, it can be used to track usage, measure compliance, and optimize software costs.

**Assessment:** The assessment phase involves analyzing the software inventory data to identify potential compliance issues, redundant software, and optimization opportunities. During this phase, the SAM team typically uses software asset management tools to help identify discrepancies between the software inventory and licensing records. This phase also includes reviewing the organization's software usage and identifying opportunities to optimize software licensing and usage to reduce costs and improve compliance. The output of the assessment phase is a report that outlines the compliance risks, optimization opportunities, and recommended actions.

**Optimization:** Software optimization is the process of maximizing the value of an organization's software assets while minimizing the costs. This can be achieved by implementing processes to reduce software costs, eliminate redundant software, and optimize licensing agreements. This may involve negotiating better license agreements with vendors, reducing the number of unused or underused licenses, and implementing license management policies to ensure that software usage is compliant with the licensing agreements. It may also involve identifying opportunities to switch to less expensive or open-source software, virtualizing software applications to reduce hardware requirements, and centralizing software procurement to take advantage of volume discounts.

**Management:** Software Asset Management (SAM) includes a management process that involves maintaining an accurate software inventory, including newly deployed software, and ensuring compliance with licensing agreements. This involves ongoing monitoring and management of the software usage, license entitlements, and license usage data to ensure that the software is used in accordance with the licensing agreements and compliance standards. The management process also includes optimizing license agreements, reducing software costs, and eliminating redundant software to maintain an efficient and cost-effective software environment. Additionally, the management process involves training end-users on licensing policies and procedures to ensure that they are aware of their software usage rights and responsibilities.

**Reporting:** The reporting phase of SAM involves providing regular reports to stakeholders on the status of the SAM program. These reports should include information on software inventory, license compliance, cost savings, risk mitigation, and other relevant metrics to ensure that the SAM program is meeting its objectives. The reports can also be used to identify areas where the SAM program can be improved, such as optimizing licensing agreements or reducing software costs.

**Disposal:** Disposal is an important phase in the software asset management process. It involves the proper disposal of software that is no longer needed. This includes removing the software from hardware and deleting licenses to avoid compliance issues. It's essential to ensure that the disposal is done in a secure and environmentally friendly manner.

## Software Optimization

Software optimization is the process of optimizing software usage to reduce costs, increase efficiency, and improve performance. Effective software optimization requires a comprehensive understanding of software usage patterns, license entitlements, and licensing agreements.

Software optimization can be achieved through several strategies, including:

1. **License Consolidation:** License consolidation involves consolidating multiple licenses of the S.A.M software product into a single license. This can help reduce the number of licenses required and lower costs.
2. **License Re-harvesting:** License re-harvesting involves reclaiming unused licenses and reallocating them to other users or departments. This can help optimize license usage and reduce costs.

3. **License Optimization:** License optimization involves optimizing license usage to ensure that licenses are being used in a way that aligns with business needs and licensing agreements. This can help avoid unnecessary license purchases and reduce costs.

4. **Vendor Negotiation:** Vendor negotiation involves negotiating more favorable licensing terms with software vendors. This can help reduce costs and optimize software usage.

5. **Software Retirement:** Software retirement involves retiring or decommissioning software that is no longer needed or used. This can help reduce costs and simplify software inventory management.

Effective software optimization requires ongoing monitoring of software usage and license compliance. This involves regularly monitoring license usage, identifying opportunities for license optimization, and taking appropriate action to ensure compliance with licensing agreements.

In addition to the strategies mentioned earlier, organizations can use S.A.M tools to optimize software usage. S.A.M tools can provide real-time visibility into software inventory and usage, enabling organizations to identify opportunities for license optimization and avoid unnecessary license purchases.

S.A.M tools can also provide automated license management, enabling organizations to optimize license usage and reduce costs. By automating license management tasks such as license allocation, reclamation, and optimization, S.A.M tools can help organizations achieve more efficient and cost-effective license management.

Effective software optimization requires ongoing monitoring and management of software assets. Organizations should regularly review their software usage and licensing agreements to identify opportunities for optimization and ensure compliance with licensing agreements. By following best practices for software optimization and using S.A.M tools, organizations can optimize their software usage, reduce costs, and achieve the benefits of effective software optimization.

Effective software optimization can provide several benefits to organizations, including:

1. **Reduced Costs:** Effective software optimization can help reduce costs by optimizing license usage, avoiding unnecessary license purchases, and retiring or decommissioning software that is no longer needed or used.
2. **Increased Efficiency:** Effective software optimization can help improve efficiency by ensuring that software is being used in a way

that aligns with business needs and licensing agreements.

3. **Improved Performance:** Effective software optimization can help improve software performance by ensuring that software is up to date and free from bugs and security vulnerabilities.

4. **Better Decision Making:** Effective software optimization can provide organizations with the information they need to make informed decisions about software usage, license management, and procurement.

5. **Enhanced Security:** Effective software optimization can help enhance software security by ensuring that software is up to date and free from security vulnerabilities.

To achieve effective software optimization, organizations should follow some best practices, such as:

1. **Establish a S.A.M Strategy:** Organizations should establish a S.A.M strategy that includes clear goals and objectives, and a plan for how software assets will be managed and optimized.

2. **Use S.A.M Tools:** S.A.M tools can provide real-time visibility into software inventory and usage, enabling organizations to identify opportunities for license optimization and avoid unnecessary license purchases.

3. **Regularly Review Software Usage:** Organizations should regularly review their software usage to identify opportunities for license optimization and ensure compliance with licensing agreements.

4. **Optimize License Usage:** Organizations should optimize license usage by ensuring that licenses are being used in a way that aligns with business needs and licensing agreements.

5. **Retire or Decommission Unused Software:** Organizations should retire or decommission software that is no longer needed or used to simplify software inventory management and reduce costs.

6. **Negotiate Favorable Licensing Terms:** Organizations should negotiate more favorable licensing terms with software vendors to reduce costs and optimize software usage.

7. **Maintain Compliance:** Organizations should maintain compliance with licensing agreements to avoid legal and financial risks associated with non-compliance.

In conclusion, effective software optimization is critical for managing software assets and ensuring that they are being used in a way that aligns with business needs and licensing agreements. By following best practices for software optimization and using S.A.M tools, organizations can optimize their software usage, reduce costs, and achieve the benefits of effective software optimization.

## S.A.M Strategy

A S.A.M strategy is a comprehensive plan that outlines how an organization will manage its software assets, from acquisition to retirement. A S.A.M strategy should include clear goals and objectives, a plan for how software assets will be managed and optimized, and a roadmap for how the strategy will be implemented.

The following are some key elements of a S.A.M strategy:

1. **Goals and Objectives:** A S.A.M strategy should have clear goals and objectives that are aligned with the organization's overall goals and objectives. The goals and objectives should be specific, measurable, achievable, relevant, and time-bound.

2. **Inventory Management:** A S.A.M strategy should include a plan for managing software inventory, including the acquisition, installation, and tracking of software assets. This plan should ensure that software inventory is accurate, up to date, and reflects the organization's current software usage.

3. **License Management:** A S.A.M strategy should include a plan for managing software licenses, including the acquisition, allocation, and optimization of licenses. This plan should ensure

that licenses are being used in a way that aligns with business needs and licensing agreements.

4. **Compliance Management:** A S.A.M strategy should include a plan for managing compliance with licensing agreements and other legal requirements. This plan should ensure that the organization is in compliance with licensing agreements and is avoiding legal and financial risks associated with non-compliance.

5. **Vendor Management:** A S.A.M strategy should include a plan for managing software vendors, including the negotiation of more favorable licensing terms and the resolution of any vendor disputes.

6. **S.A.M Processes and Procedures:** A S.A.M strategy should include a plan for implementing S.A.M processes and procedures, such as license allocation, reclamation, and optimization. This plan should ensure that S.A.M processes and procedures are being followed and that they are delivering the intended benefits.

7. **S.A.M Tools:** A S.A.M strategy should include a plan for selecting and implementing S.A.M tools. This plan should ensure that the selected S.A.M tools are appropriate for the organization's needs and that they are providing the intended benefits.

To develop an effective S.A.M strategy, organizations should follow some best practices, such as:

1. **Establish S.A.M Policies and Procedures:** Organizations should establish policies and procedures that provide guidance on how software assets should be managed and optimized. This should include guidelines for acquiring, installing, and tracking software assets, as well as procedures for managing licenses and ensuring compliance with licensing agreements.

2. **Conduct a S.A.M Assessment:** Organizations should conduct a S.A.M assessment to evaluate their current S.A.M practices and identify areas for improvement. This assessment should include a review of software inventory, licensing agreements, compliance practices, and software usage patterns.

3. **Set Clear Goals and Objectives:** Organizations should set clear goals and objectives for their S.A.M strategy, including targets for reducing costs, optimizing license usage, and improving compliance practices.

4. **Align S.A.M Strategy with Business Goals:** Organizations should ensure that their S.A.M strategy is aligned with their overall business goals and objectives. This can help ensure that S.A.M practices are supporting the organization's strategic priorities.

5. **Establish a S.A.M Team:** Organizations should establish a dedicated S.A.M team that is

responsible for implementing and managing the S.A.M strategy. This team should include representatives from IT, procurement, legal, and other relevant departments.

6. **Use S.A.M Tools:** Organizations should use S.A.M tools to automate inventory management tasks, provide real-time visibility into license usage, and optimize license usage.

7. **Regularly Review and Update the S.A.M Strategy:** Organizations should regularly review and update their S.A.M strategy to ensure that it is meeting the organization's evolving needs and priorities.

Effective implementation of a S.A.M strategy requires a structured approach to software asset management that is supported by best practices and S.A.M tools. The following are some best practices that organizations can follow to ensure the effective implementation of their S.A.M strategy:

1. **Establish S.A.M Roles and Responsibilities:** Organizations should establish clear roles and responsibilities for S.A.M activities. This should include identifying who is responsible for software acquisition, inventory management, license management, and compliance management.

2. **Educate Employees:** Organizations should educate employees on the importance of S.A.M

and how it benefits the organization. This should include providing training on S.A.M policies and procedures and best practices for software usage.

3. **Automate S.A.M Processes:** Organizations should use S.A.M tools to automate S.A.M processes and reduce the time and effort required for S.A.M activities. S.A.M tools can help automate inventory management, license management, and compliance management.

4. **Monitor Software Usage:** Organizations should regularly monitor software usage to identify opportunities for license optimization and ensure compliance with licensing agreements. This can help avoid unnecessary license purchases and reduce costs.

5. **Align S.A.M with Business Objectives:** Organizations should align S.A.M with their overall business objectives. This can help ensure that S.A.M practices are supporting the organization's strategic priorities and are contributing to the achievement of business goals.

6. **Conduct Regular Audits:** Organizations should conduct regular S.A.M audits to ensure compliance with licensing agreements and identify opportunities for improvement.

7. **Engage with Vendors:** Organizations should engage with software vendors to negotiate

more favorable licensing terms and resolve any vendor disputes.

S.A.M tools can provide significant benefits in terms of optimizing software usage, reducing costs, and mitigating legal and security risks. The following are some key benefits of using S.A.M tools:

1. **Real-time Visibility into Software Inventory:** S.A.M tools can provide real-time visibility into software inventory, enabling organizations to identify opportunities for license optimization and avoid unnecessary license purchases.
2. **License Optimization:** S.A.M tools can help optimize license usage by ensuring that licenses are being used in a way that aligns with business needs and licensing agreements. This can help avoid unnecessary license purchases and reduce costs.
3. **Compliance Management:** S.A.M tools can help organizations manage compliance with licensing agreements and avoid legal and financial risks associated with non-compliance.
4. **License Re-harvesting:** S.A.M tools can help organizations reclaim unused licenses and reallocate them to other users or departments, optimizing license usage and reducing costs.
5. **Vendor Management:** S.A.M tools can help organizations manage relationships with software vendors, negotiate more favorable

licensing terms, and resolve any vendor disputes.

6. **Automated Reporting:** S.A.M tools can provide automated reporting on software usage and license compliance, enabling organizations to quickly identify opportunities for optimization and ensure compliance with licensing agreements.

7. **Cost Savings:** S.A.M tools can help organizations reduce costs by optimizing license usage, avoiding unnecessary license purchases, and retiring or decommissioning software that is no longer needed or used.

In conclusion, S.A.M tools can provide significant benefits to organizations in terms of optimizing software usage, reducing costs, and mitigating legal and security risks. By using S.A.M tools, organizations can automate inventory management tasks, provide real-time visibility into license usage, optimize license usage, and reduce costs. S.A.M tools can also help organizations maintain compliance with licensing agreements and manage relationships with software vendors.

## Software Cost Reduction

Software cost reduction is the process of identifying and implementing strategies to reduce software-related costs. Effective software cost reduction requires a comprehensive understanding of software usage patterns, license entitlements, and licensing agreements.

The following are some strategies that organizations can use to reduce software costs:

1. **Software Consolidation:** Software consolidation involves consolidating multiple software applications into a single application, reducing the number of licenses required and lowering costs.

2. **License Re-Harvesting:** License re-harvesting involves reclaiming unused licenses and reallocating them to other users or departments, optimizing license usage and reducing costs.

3. **License Optimization:** License optimization involves optimizing license usage to ensure that licenses are being used in a way that aligns with business needs and licensing agreements. This can help avoid unnecessary license purchases and reduce costs.

4. **Vendor Negotiation:** Vendor negotiation involves negotiating more favorable licensing terms with software vendors. This can help reduce costs and optimize software usage.

5. **Software Retirement:** Software retirement involves retiring or decommissioning software that is no longer needed or used. This can help

reduce costs and simplify software inventory management.

6. **Open Source Alternatives:** Organizations can consider using open source software as an alternative to proprietary software, which can help reduce software licensing costs.

Effective software cost reduction requires ongoing monitoring of software usage and license compliance. This involves regularly monitoring license usage, identifying opportunities for license optimization, and taking appropriate action to ensure compliance with licensing agreements.

To achieve effective software cost reduction, organizations should follow some best practices, such as:

1. **Conduct a Software Audit:** Organizations should conduct a software audit to identify software assets, usage patterns, and license entitlements. This can help identify opportunities for license optimization and software consolidation.

2. **Establish a Software Cost Reduction Strategy:** Organizations should establish a software cost reduction strategy that includes clear goals and objectives, a plan for managing software inventory and licenses, and a roadmap for implementation.

3. **Regularly Review Software Usage:** Organizations should regularly review their software usage to identify opportunities for license optimization and ensure compliance with licensing agreements.

4. **Negotiate Favorable Licensing Terms:** Organizations should negotiate more favorable licensing terms with software vendors to reduce costs and optimize software usage.

5. **Retire or Decommission Unused Software:** Organizations should retire or decommission software that is no longer needed or used to simplify software inventory management and reduce costs.

6. **Use Open Source Alternatives:** Organizations can consider using open source software as an alternative to proprietary software, which can help reduce software licensing costs.

7. **Implement License Management:** Organizations should implement license management processes to optimize license usage and reduce costs.

Effective software cost reduction also requires a proactive approach to software asset management (S.A.M) that is supported by best practices and S.A.M tools. The following are some best practices that organizations can follow to ensure the effective reduction of software costs:

1. **Conduct a Cost-Benefit Analysis:** Organizations should conduct a cost-benefit analysis to determine the return on investment (ROI) of software assets. This can help identify opportunities for cost reduction and optimization.

2. **Use S.A.M Tools:** S.A.M tools can provide real-time visibility into software inventory and usage, enabling organizations to identify opportunities for license optimization and avoid unnecessary license purchases.

3. **Monitor Software Usage:** Organizations should regularly monitor software usage to identify opportunities for license optimization and ensure compliance with licensing agreements. This can help avoid unnecessary license purchases and reduce costs.

4. **Align S.A.M with Business Objectives:** Organizations should ensure that their S.A.M practices are aligned with their overall business objectives. This can help ensure that S.A.M practices are supporting the organization's strategic priorities and are contributing to the achievement of business goals.

5. **Maintain Compliance:** Organizations should maintain compliance with licensing agreements to avoid legal and financial risks associated with non-compliance.

6. **Negotiate Favorable Licensing Terms:** Organizations should negotiate more favorable licensing terms with software vendors to reduce costs and optimize software usage.
7. **Regularly Review and Update S.A.M Strategy:** Organizations should regularly review and update their S.A.M strategy to ensure that it is meeting the organization's evolving needs and priorities.

Another important aspect of software cost reduction is to ensure that software procurement is done in an efficient and cost-effective manner. The following are some best practices that organizations can follow for efficient software procurement:

1. **Create a Software Procurement Policy:** Organizations should create a software procurement policy that outlines the procurement process, vendor selection criteria, and purchasing authority.
2. **Evaluate Software Alternatives:** Organizations should evaluate software alternatives to ensure that the software selected is the best fit for their needs and provides the best value for money.
3. **Leverage Volume Licensing:** Organizations can leverage volume licensing to negotiate more favorable licensing terms and reduce costs.

4. **Consolidate Purchases:** Organizations should consolidate software purchases to reduce costs and simplify software procurement.
5. **Engage with Vendors:** Organizations should engage with software vendors to negotiate more favorable licensing terms and resolve any vendor disputes.
6. **Use a Centralized Procurement System**: Organizations should use a centralized procurement system to manage software procurement and reduce administrative costs.
7. **Monitor Procurement Costs:** Organizations should monitor software procurement costs to identify opportunities for cost reduction and optimization.

In conclusion, efficient software procurement is critical for effective software cost reduction. By following best practices for software procurement, such as creating a procurement policy, evaluating software alternatives, leveraging volume licensing, consolidating purchases, engaging with vendors, using a centralized procurement system, and monitoring procurement costs, organizations can optimize their software procurement process, reduce costs, and achieve the benefits of efficient software procurement.

## Software Risk Mitigation

Software risk mitigation is the process of identifying, assessing, and managing risks associated with software assets to reduce the probability and impact of negative outcomes. Effective software risk mitigation requires a comprehensive understanding of software usage patterns, licensing agreements, and security risks.

The following are some strategies that organizations can use to mitigate software-related risks:

1. **Conduct a Software Risk Assessment:** Organizations should conduct a software risk assessment to identify software-related risks and develop strategies to mitigate these risks. This should include a review of software inventory, licensing agreements, and compliance practices.

2. **Maintain Compliance with Licensing Agreements:** Organizations should maintain compliance with licensing agreements to avoid legal and financial risks associated with non-compliance.

3. **Implement Software Security Controls:** Organizations should implement software security controls, such as firewalls, anti-virus software, and intrusion detection systems, to reduce the risk of security breaches and cyber-attacks.

4. Regularly Patch and Update Software: Organizations should regularly patch and update software to address known

vulnerabilities and reduce the risk of security breaches and cyber-attacks.

5. **Use S.A.M Tools:** S.A.M tools can help organizations manage software inventory, optimize license usage, and maintain compliance with licensing agreements, reducing the risk of legal and financial risks associated with non-compliance.

6. **Educate Employees:** Organizations should educate employees on the importance of software security and best practices for software usage. This can help reduce the risk of security breaches and cyber-attacks caused by human error.

7. **Use Open Source Software:** Organizations can consider using open source software as an alternative to proprietary software, which can reduce the risk of security breaches and cyber-attacks.

Effective software risk mitigation also requires a proactive approach to software asset management (S.A.M) that is supported by best practices and S.A.M tools. The following are some best practices that organizations can follow to ensure the effective mitigation of software-related risks:

1. **Create a S.A.M Plan:** Organizations should create a S.A.M plan that includes a risk

assessment, risk mitigation strategies, and a roadmap for implementation.

2. **Use S.A.M Tools:** S.A.M tools can provide real-time visibility into software inventory and usage, enabling organizations to identify security risks and mitigate them in a timely manner.

3. **Regularly Monitor Software Usage:** Organizations should regularly monitor software usage to identify security risks and take appropriate action to mitigate them.

4. **Establish a Software Security Policy:** Organizations should establish a software security policy that outlines best practices for software usage, access control, and data protection.

5. **Educate Employees:** Organizations should educate employees on the importance of software security and best practices for software usage, access control, and data protection.

6. **Conduct Regular Security Audits:** Organizations should conduct regular security audits to identify vulnerabilities and take appropriate action to address them.

7. **Maintain Compliance with Regulatory Standards:** Organizations should maintain compliance with regulatory standards, such as the General Data Protection Regulation (GDPR),

to avoid legal and financial risks associated with non-compliance.

In addition to the best practices mentioned above, organizations can also consider implementing additional measures to further mitigate software-related risks. The following are some additional measures that organizations can consider:

1. **Implement Multi-Factor Authentication:** Organizations can consider implementing multi-factor authentication to provide an additional layer of security for accessing software applications and data.
2. **Implement Data Encryption:** Organizations can consider implementing data encryption to protect sensitive data from unauthorized access.
3. **Perform Regular Backups:** Organizations should perform regular backups of critical data to ensure that data can be restored in the event of a security breach or other negative event.
4. **Implement a Disaster Recovery Plan:** Organizations should implement a disaster recovery plan to ensure that critical systems and data can be restored in the event of a security breach, natural disaster, or other negative event.
5. **Use Cloud-based Solutions:** Organizations can consider using cloud-based solutions that

provide enhanced security and reliability compared to on-premises solutions.

6. **Implement Change Management Processes:** Organizations should implement change management processes to ensure that software updates and changes are implemented in a controlled and secure manner.

7. Regularly Test and Validate Security Controls: Organizations should regularly test and validate software security controls to ensure that they are working as

Finally, it's important for organizations to continuously monitor and update their software risk mitigation strategies to ensure that they are effective and aligned with the organization's evolving needs and priorities. This involves regularly reviewing and updating the S.A.M plan, conducting regular risk assessments, and monitoring software usage and compliance practices.

By continuously monitoring and updating software risk mitigation strategies, organizations can adapt to changing circumstances and emerging threats, and ensure that they are effectively managing software-related risks. This can help mitigate the negative impact of software-related risks, reduce costs associated with software security breaches and non-compliance, and enable organizations to achieve the benefits of effective software asset management.

In summary, software risk mitigation is a critical aspect of software asset management, which involves identifying, assessing, and managing risks associated with software assets. Effective software risk mitigation requires a comprehensive understanding of software usage patterns, licensing agreements, and security risks, and involves following best practices and implementing additional measures to mitigate software-related risks. By continuously monitoring and updating software risk mitigation strategies, organizations can adapt to changing circumstances and emerging threats, and ensure that they are effectively managing software-related risks.

## S.A.M Plan

A S.A.M plan is a comprehensive strategy that outlines an organization's approach to software asset management (S.A.M). It should include the following elements:

1. **Goals and Objectives:** The S.A.M plan should clearly outline the organization's goals and objectives related to S.A.M, including reducing costs, optimizing software usage, and mitigating software-related risks.
2. **Scope:** The S.A.M plan should define the scope of S.A.M activities, including the software assets that are included in the plan and the geographic locations that are covered.

3. **Roles and Responsibilities:** The S.A.M plan should clearly define the roles and responsibilities of the personnel involved in S.A.M, including the S.A.M team, software users, and software vendors.
4. **S.A.M Processes:** The S.A.M plan should outline the processes and procedures that will be used to manage software assets, including software procurement, software deployment, license optimization, software retirement, and compliance management.
5. **S.A.M Tools:** The S.A.M plan should identify the S.A.M tools that will be used to manage software assets, including tools for software inventory management, license optimization, and compliance management.
6. **S.A.M Metrics:** The S.A.M plan should define the metrics that will be used to measure the success of S.A.M activities, including cost savings, license optimization, and compliance rates.
7. **S.A.M Roadmap:** The S.A.M plan should include a roadmap for implementing S.A.M activities, including a timeline for completing key activities and milestones.

An effective S.A.M plan should be aligned with the organization's overall business objectives and should take into account the organization's software usage patterns, licensing agreements, and security risks. It should be regularly reviewed and updated to ensure that it remains relevant and effective.

To create a S.A.M plan, organizations should follow these steps:

1. **Conduct a Software Audit:** The first step is to conduct a software audit to identify all software assets used by the organization, including proprietary and open source software. This will provide an accurate picture of the organization's software usage patterns and will inform the development of the S.A.M plan.

2. **Identify Goals and Objectives:** The next step is to identify the goals and objectives of the S.A.M plan, such as reducing software costs, optimizing software usage, and mitigating software-related risks. These goals should be aligned with the organization's overall business objectives.

3. **Define the Scope:** The S.A.M plan should clearly define the scope of S.A.M activities, including the software assets that are included in the plan and the geographic locations that are covered.

4. **Identify Roles and Responsibilities:** The S.A.M plan should clearly define the roles and responsibilities of the personnel involved in S.A.M, including the S.A.M team, software users, and software vendors.

5. **Develop S.A.M Processes:** The S.A.M plan should define the processes and procedures that will be used to manage software assets, including software procurement, software deployment, license optimization, software retirement, and compliance management.
6. **Identify S.A.M Tools:** The S.A.M plan should identify the S.A.M tools that will be used to manage software assets, including tools for software inventory management, license optimization, and compliance management.
7. **Define S.A.M Metrics:** The S.A.M plan should define the metrics that will be used to measure the success of S.A.M activities, including cost savings, license optimization, and compliance rates.
8. **Develop a S.A.M Roadmap:** The S.A.M plan should include a roadmap for implementing S.A.M activities, including a timeline for completing key activities and milestones.

To effectively implement a S.A.M plan, organizations should also follow best practices for software asset management. Some best practices to follow include:

1. **Regularly Update Software Inventory:** Organizations should regularly update their software inventory to ensure that it is accurate and up-to-date. This will enable organizations to

identify all software assets in use and reduce the risk of non-compliance.

2. **Monitor Software Usage:** Organizations should monitor software usage to ensure that licenses are being used efficiently and effectively. This can help identify underused licenses and opportunities for license optimization.

3. **Automate License Management:** Organizations should consider using software tools to automate license management processes, such as license tracking and renewal notifications.

4. **Educate Software Users:** Organizations should educate software users on software usage policies and best practices to reduce the risk of non-compliance and improve software usage efficiency.

5. **Conduct Regular License Audits:** Organizations should conduct regular license audits to ensure that software usage is compliant with licensing agreements and to identify opportunities for cost savings.

6. **Implement Effective Software Procurement Practices:** Organizations should implement effective software procurement practices, including negotiating favorable licensing terms and consolidating purchases, to reduce costs and ensure compliance with licensing agreements.

7. **Maintain Compliance with Software Licensing Agreements:** Organizations should maintain compliance with software licensing agreements to avoid legal and financial risks associated with non-compliance.

In addition to the best practices outlined above, there are several other considerations that organizations should keep in mind when implementing a S.A.M plan. These include:

1. **Cultural Change:** Organizations should recognize that implementing a S.A.M plan may require a cultural change, including changes to processes and the adoption of new technologies. It is important to involve all stakeholders in the process and provide sufficient training and support to facilitate the transition.

2. **Vendor Management:** Effective vendor management is critical to the success of a S.A.M plan. Organizations should establish strong relationships with software vendors and ensure that they understand the organization's software usage requirements and licensing agreements.

3. **Data Security:** Effective S.A.M requires the collection and analysis of sensitive data, such as software usage data and licensing agreements. Organizations should take appropriate

measures to ensure the security and privacy of this data, including implementing appropriate data access controls, data encryption, and data backup procedures.

4. **Compliance Monitoring:** Effective S.A.M requires ongoing monitoring of software usage and compliance practices. Organizations should establish regular compliance monitoring processes to identify non-compliance and take appropriate corrective action.

5. **Continuous Improvement:** Effective S.A.M is an ongoing process that requires continuous improvement. Organizations should regularly review and update their S.A.M plan and practices to ensure that they remain effective and aligned with the organization's evolving needs and priorities.

In conclusion, effective implementation of a S.A.M plan requires consideration of a range of factors, including cultural change, vendor management, data security, compliance monitoring, and continuous improvement. By taking these factors into account and following best practices for software asset management, organizations can effectively manage their software assets, reduce costs, optimize software usage, and mitigate software-related risks.

## S.A.M Metrics

S.A.M metrics are key performance indicators that measure the success of an organization's software asset management (S.A.M) activities. They provide valuable insights into the effectiveness of S.A.M processes, and can help organizations identify areas for improvement and optimize software usage and cost. Some common S.A.M metrics include:

12. **License Compliance Rate:** This metric measures the percentage of software licenses that are in compliance with licensing agreements. A high compliance rate indicates effective license management and reduced risk of non-compliance.

13. **License Utilization Rate:** This metric measures the percentage of software licenses that are actively in use. A high utilization rate indicates effective license optimization and reduced costs associated with underutilized licenses.

14. **Cost Savings:** This metric measures the amount of cost savings achieved through S.A.M activities, such as reducing software licensing costs, optimizing software usage, and avoiding penalties associated with non-compliance.

15. **Total Cost of Ownership (TCO):** This metric measures the total cost of software ownership, including acquisition, deployment, maintenance, and retirement costs. A low TCO indicates effective software asset management

and reduced costs associated with software ownership.

16. **Software Asset Inventory Accuracy:** This metric measures the accuracy of the software asset inventory, including the completeness and accuracy of the information about software assets. High inventory accuracy indicates effective software asset management and reduced risk of non-compliance.

17. **User Satisfaction:** This metric measures user satisfaction with software asset management processes and tools. A high satisfaction rate indicates effective software asset management and improved software usage efficiency.

18. **Risk Reduction:** This metric measures the reduction in risk associated with software asset management, such as the reduction in security risks, non-compliance risks, and financial risks associated with software licensing.

To effectively use S.A.M metrics, organizations should follow these best practices:

1. **Define Clear Goals:** Organizations should define clear goals for their S.A.M activities, and use S.A.M metrics to track progress towards these goals. This will ensure that the metrics are aligned with the organization's overall objectives.

2. **Identify Key Performance Indicators (KPIs):** Organizations should identify the KPIs that are most relevant to their S.A.M activities and goals, and focus on tracking these metrics. This will ensure that the metrics are actionable and relevant.

3. **Collect Accurate Data:** Organizations should collect accurate and reliable data on software usage, licensing agreements, and software asset inventory, in order to provide an accurate picture of the organization's software asset management activities.

4. **Analyze and Report Metrics:** Organizations should analyze and report S.A.M metrics on a regular basis, in order to identify areas for improvement and make data-driven decisions. This will help ensure that S.A.M activities are effective and efficient.

5. **Act on Insights:** Organizations should use S.A.M metrics to gain insights into areas for improvement, and take appropriate action to address these areas. This will help ensure that S.A.M activities are continuously improving and optimizing software usage and cost.

By following these best practices, organizations can effectively use S.A.M metrics to optimize software usage and cost, reduce risks associated with software asset management, and improve user satisfaction.

**List Software Asset Management KPIs**

Here are some key performance indicators (KPIs) for Software Asset Management (SAM):

1. **License compliance rate:** The percentage of software licenses that are in compliance with licensing agreements.
2. **License utilization rate:** The percentage of licenses that are currently in use, compared to the total number of licenses owned.
3. **License spend optimization:** The amount of money saved by optimizing license usage and negotiating better licensing agreements.
4. **Reduction in compliance risks:** The decrease in risks related to license compliance and software audits.
5. **Reduction in software waste:** The amount of software that has been identified as redundant or unnecessary and removed, resulting in cost savings.
6. **Time to complete audits:** The amount of time it takes to complete a software audit, from start to finish.
7. **Software deployment time:** The time it takes to deploy new software or updates to existing software, from the time of request to the time of installation.

8. **License tracking accuracy:** The percentage of licenses that are accurately tracked and accounted for in the SAM system.
9. **Cost savings through vendor management:** The amount of money saved through effective vendor management, such as negotiating better pricing or reducing vendor lock-in.
10. **User satisfaction with software availability:** The level of satisfaction among users with the availability and accessibility of the software they need to perform their job functions.

In addition to the best practices outlined above, there are several other considerations that organizations should keep in mind when using S.A.M metrics. These include:

1. **Benchmarking:** Organizations should benchmark their S.A.M metrics against industry best practices and their own historical performance, in order to identify areas for improvement and set realistic targets.
2. **Data Visualization:** Organizations should use data visualization tools to help make S.A.M metrics more accessible and understandable. This can help users more easily interpret the data and gain insights into S.A.M performance.
3. **Integration:** Organizations should consider integrating S.A.M metrics into other performance management systems, such as

financial reporting or IT service management, in order to provide a more comprehensive picture of organizational performance.

4. **Continuous Improvement:** S.A.M metrics should be used as a tool for continuous improvement, and organizations should continuously monitor and update their S.A.M metrics to ensure that they remain relevant and effective.

5. **Executive Support:** Executive support is critical to the success of S.A.M metrics, as it helps ensure that S.A.M activities are aligned with overall business objectives and that adequate resources are allocated to S.A.M initiatives.

In addition to the best practices and considerations outlined above, there are also several specific S.A.M metrics that organizations may want to track to gain more granular insights into their software asset management activities. These include:

1. **Software License Cost Per User:** This metric measures the cost of software licenses per user. By tracking this metric over time, organizations can identify trends in software licensing costs and identify opportunities for cost savings.

2. **Software License Renewal Rate:** This metric measures the percentage of software licenses that are renewed on time. By tracking this

metric, organizations can identify areas for improvement in license renewal processes.

3. **Software License Utilization by Department:** This metric measures software license utilization by department, allowing organizations to identify departments with underutilized software licenses and opportunities for optimization.

4. **Software License Compliance by Vendor:** This metric measures software license compliance rates by vendor, allowing organizations to identify vendors with higher compliance rates and identify opportunities for improving compliance rates with other vendors.

5. **Software License Compliance by Region:** This metric measures software license compliance rates by region, allowing organizations to identify regions with higher compliance rates and identify opportunities for improving compliance rates in other regions.

6. **Software License Cost Savings by Optimization:** This metric measures the cost savings achieved through license optimization activities, such as identifying and retiring underutilized licenses. By tracking this metric, organizations can identify the ROI of their license optimization efforts.

7. **Software License Compliance Audit Pass Rate:** This metric measures the pass rate of software

license compliance audits, allowing organizations to identify areas for improvement in compliance management processes.

In conclusion, by tracking these specific S.A.M metrics in addition to the more general S.A.M metrics outlined earlier, organizations can gain more granular insights into their software asset management activities and identify opportunities for improvement and cost savings. By using these metrics to drive continuous improvement in S.A.M activities, organizations can optimize software usage and cost, reduce risks associated with software asset management, and improve user satisfaction.

## S.A.M Roadmap

A software S.A.M roadmap is a plan that outlines the steps an organization needs to take to achieve effective software asset management (S.A.M). The roadmap should include a detailed timeline, specific goals and objectives, and actionable steps to be taken to achieve those goals. Here are the key components of a S.A.M roadmap:

1. **Assessment:** The first step in creating a S.A.M roadmap is to assess the organization's current software asset management practices, including the software asset inventory, software usage, licensing agreements, and compliance management processes. This assessment

should identify areas for improvement and provide a baseline for measuring progress.

2. **Goal Setting:** Once the assessment is complete, the organization should set specific goals and objectives for its S.A.M activities. These goals should be aligned with the organization's overall business objectives and should be measurable and achievable within a defined timeframe.

3. **Plan Development:** With goals in place, the organization should develop a detailed plan for achieving those goals. This plan should include specific tasks and timelines for each goal and should identify the resources needed to execute the plan.

4. **Implementation:** Once the plan is developed, the organization should begin implementing the plan, following the specific tasks and timelines identified in the plan. This may involve updating the software asset inventory, optimizing software usage, renegotiating licensing agreements, and improving compliance management processes.

5. **Metrics and Monitoring:** Throughout the implementation phase, the organization should track specific S.A.M metrics to measure progress towards its goals. The organization should also regularly monitor its S.A.M practices and processes, identifying areas for

improvement and taking corrective action as needed.

6. **Continuous Improvement:** S.A.M is an ongoing process, and the organization should continuously review and update its S.A.M roadmap and practices to ensure that they remain effective and aligned with the organization's evolving needs and priorities.

In addition to the steps outlined above, there are several other considerations that organizations should keep in mind when developing a software S.A.M roadmap. These include:

1. **Executive Buy-In:** Effective S.A.M requires executive support and buy-in, as it involves significant resource allocation and cultural change. It is critical to involve executives in the development of the S.A.M roadmap and gain their support for the plan.

2. **Stakeholder Engagement:** Effective S.A.M requires stakeholder engagement, including IT staff, end-users, and software vendors. It is important to involve all stakeholders in the development of the S.A.M roadmap and regularly communicate progress and outcomes to them.

3. **Risk Management:** Effective S.A.M involves risk management, including the identification and mitigation of non-compliance and security risks

associated with software usage. It is important to include risk management strategies in the S.A.M roadmap.

4. **Vendor Management:** Effective S.A.M requires effective vendor management, including negotiating favorable licensing terms and maintaining positive relationships with software vendors. It is important to include vendor management strategies in the S.A.M roadmap.

5. **Resource Allocation:** Effective S.A.M requires resource allocation, including financial, technical, and human resources. It is important to identify the resources needed to execute the S.A.M roadmap and ensure that they are allocated appropriately.

To further support the development and execution of a successful software S.A.M roadmap, organizations should also consider the following best practices:

1. **Standardization:** Organizations should strive for standardization in their S.A.M practices, including the use of common tools, processes, and metrics. This will help ensure consistency and reduce the complexity of S.A.M activities.

2. **Automation:** Organizations should consider automating S.A.M activities, such as software asset inventory management, compliance monitoring, and license optimization. This can help improve the accuracy and efficiency of

S.A.M activities and reduce the risk of human error.

3. **Integration:** Organizations should consider integrating S.A.M activities with other IT and business processes, such as IT service management, financial management, and procurement. This can help provide a more comprehensive view of the organization's performance and reduce duplication of effort.

4. **Training:** Organizations should provide training and support to staff involved in S.A.M activities, in order to ensure that they have the necessary skills and knowledge to perform their roles effectively.

5. **Continuous Communication:** Organizations should ensure that S.A.M activities and outcomes are communicated regularly and effectively to all stakeholders. This can help build support for S.A.M activities and promote collaboration and engagement.

In addition to the best practices outlined earlier, organizations should also consider the following tips for optimizing their software asset management:

1. **Conduct Regular Audits:** Conducting regular audits of software assets, licenses, and compliance can help organizations identify areas for optimization, cost savings, and risk reduction.

2. **Use S.A.M Tools:** There are a wide variety of S.A.M tools available that can help organizations automate software inventory management, license compliance, and optimization processes. Implementing these tools can help improve the efficiency and accuracy of S.A.M activities.

3. **Monitor Usage:** Organizations should monitor software usage to identify underutilized licenses and opportunities for optimization. This can help reduce licensing costs and improve overall software usage efficiency.

4. **Negotiate Favorable Terms:** Organizations should negotiate favorable licensing terms with software vendors, such as volume discounts, multi-year contracts, and more flexible licensing models. This can help reduce licensing costs and improve compliance management.

5. **Adopt Cloud-Based Solutions:** Cloud-based software solutions can offer more flexible licensing models and allow for more effective license management. This can help reduce licensing costs and improve software usage efficiency.

6. **Educate Users:** Educating users on the importance of software asset management and their role in S.A.M activities can help improve compliance and reduce the risk of non-compliance.

7. **Centralize S.A.M Activities:** Centralizing S.A.M activities within an organization can help improve consistency and reduce duplication of effort. This can help improve the efficiency and accuracy of S.A.M activities.

In conclusion, by following these tips for optimizing software asset management, organizations can achieve more effective and efficient S.A.M practices, reduce licensing costs, and improve compliance management. Combining these tips with the best practices outlined earlier can help organizations create a comprehensive and effective software asset management program.

## Software Procurement

Software procurement is the process of acquiring software products or services for an organization. It involves identifying the software requirements, evaluating the options available in the market, selecting the most suitable solution, negotiating the contract, and finalizing the purchase. The procurement process can include activities such as market research, supplier identification, request for proposal (RFP), evaluation, negotiation, contract management, and implementation. The goal of software procurement is to acquire the necessary software products or services that meet the organization's requirements and provide value for money. Effective software procurement can help organizations manage costs, reduce risk, and improve overall performance.

The procurement process typically involves the following steps:

1. **Identify Software Needs:** The first step in software procurement is to identify the software needs of the organization. This may involve gathering requirements from end-users, IT staff, and other stakeholders.

2. **Research and Evaluate Software:** Once the software needs have been identified, the organization should research and evaluate software options that meet those needs. This may involve reviewing vendor websites, attending product demos, and consulting with industry analysts.

3. **Develop a Business Case:** Once a software option has been identified, the organization should develop a business case for the purchase of the software. The business case should include a cost-benefit analysis, a risk assessment, and an evaluation of alternatives.

4. **Obtain Approvals:** Once the business case has been developed, the organization should obtain the necessary approvals for the purchase of the software. This may involve obtaining approval from the budget office, procurement office, and other stakeholders.

5. **Negotiate Contracts:** Once approvals have been obtained, the organization should negotiate a contract with the software vendor. This may involve negotiating licensing terms, service level agreements, and pricing.
6. **Manage Procurement:** Once the contract has been negotiated, the organization should manage the procurement process, including the purchase of the software and the implementation of the software.
7. **Monitor and Evaluate Performance:** After the software has been implemented, the organization should monitor and evaluate the performance of the software to ensure that it is meeting the needs of the organization.

In addition to the steps outlined earlier, there are several other considerations that organizations should keep in mind when procuring software:

1. **Compliance:** Organizations should ensure that the software being procured is in compliance with relevant laws, regulations, and licensing requirements. This may involve reviewing licensing agreements, understanding usage restrictions, and monitoring compliance with licensing terms.
2. **Security:** Organizations should consider the security implications of the software being procured. This may involve assessing the

software for potential vulnerabilities, understanding the vendor's security policies and practices, and ensuring that the software is compatible with the organization's existing security infrastructure.

3. **Integration:** Organizations should consider the compatibility of the software being procured with the organization's existing software and infrastructure. This may involve assessing the software's compatibility with existing hardware, operating systems, and other software.

4. **Support:** Organizations should ensure that the software vendor provides adequate support and maintenance for the software being procured. This may involve reviewing the vendor's support policies and practices, understanding the vendor's response times for resolving issues, and ensuring that the organization has access to the support resources needed to effectively use the software.

5. **Training:** Organizations should ensure that end-users are trained on how to effectively use the software being procured. This may involve providing training sessions or access to training resources, such as user manuals or online tutorials.

To further support the effective procurement of software, organizations should also consider the following best practices:

1. **Procurement Strategy:** Organizations should develop a procurement strategy that outlines the procurement process, identifies stakeholders, and establishes procurement goals and objectives.

2. **Vendor Management:** Organizations should establish effective vendor management practices, including evaluating vendors based on their capabilities, service level agreements, pricing, and quality of support.

3. **Contract Management:** Organizations should establish effective contract management practices, including developing standardized contract templates, negotiating favorable contract terms, and monitoring contract performance.

4. **Cost Management:** Organizations should establish effective cost management practices, including conducting cost-benefit analyses, identifying cost-saving opportunities, and optimizing software license usage.

5. **Governance:** Organizations should establish effective governance practices to ensure that software procurement aligns with overall business objectives and is in compliance with relevant policies and regulations.

In addition to the steps and best practices outlined earlier, there are several other tips that organizations should consider to optimize their software procurement process:

1. **Involve End-Users:** End-users should be involved in the software procurement process to ensure that their needs are met and that the software is user-friendly.

2. **Develop a Procurement Calendar:** Organizations should develop a procurement calendar that outlines the timing of software procurement activities to ensure that they are completed on time and within budget.

3. **Monitor Industry Trends:** Organizations should monitor industry trends in software procurement to stay up-to-date on new software offerings and emerging best practices.

4. **Leverage Existing Relationships:** Organizations should leverage existing relationships with software vendors to negotiate favorable pricing and licensing terms.

5. **Seek Expert Advice:** Organizations should seek expert advice from industry analysts or consultants to help identify the best software options and to negotiate favorable contract terms.

In conclusion, by following these tips, organizations can optimize their software procurement process and acquire software that meets their needs and provides value for the organization. Effective software procurement is critical to the success of an organization, and organizations should approach software procurement with a systematic and well-defined process that takes into account the needs of end-users, compliance, security, integration, support, and training considerations, as well as the best practices and tips outlined earlier.

Software Procurement Process

The software procurement process involves the following steps:

1. **Needs Assessment:** Identifying the software requirements of the organization.
2. **Vendor Identification:** Identifying vendors who can provide the required software.
3. **Vendor Evaluation:** Evaluating potential vendors based on their reputation, product features, and pricing.
4. **Negotiation:** Negotiating the terms of the software license agreement with the vendor.
5. **Contract Review:** Reviewing the software license agreement with legal and IT teams.
6. **Purchase:** Purchasing the software license from the selected vendor.
7. **Delivery and Installation:** Ensuring the delivery and installation of the software.

8. **Testing:** Testing the software to ensure it meets the organization's requirements.
9. **Deployment:** Deploying the software in the organization.
10. **Maintenance:** Ongoing maintenance and support of the software, which may include upgrades, patches, and bug fixes.

Procurement & Vendor management Metrics & KPIs

Here are some procurement process and vendor management metrics and KPIs that may be helpful:

1. Time-to-market for new products or services
2. Supplier lead time
3. Purchase order cycle time
4. Purchase order accuracy rate
5. Supplier quality ratings
6. Number of supplier defects or non-conformances
7. Purchase price variance
8. Cost savings from negotiations with suppliers
9. Contract compliance rate
10. Number of supplier audits conducted
11. Supplier performance against service level agreements (SLAs)
12. On-time delivery rate
13. Percentage of emergency purchases
14. Number of supplier issues escalated to management
15. Supplier innovation rate

16. Purchase requisition approval cycle time
17. Percentage of spend under management
18. Cost avoidance from early payment discounts or other savings programs
19. Supplier diversity metrics, such as number of diverse suppliers or diversity spend
20. Risk management metrics, such as supplier risk assessments or contingency plans.

It's important to note that the specific metrics and KPIs used will vary depending on the organization's priorities and goals for procurement and vendor management.

## Software Information Technology

Software Information Technology, also known as Software IT, refers to the use of software and related technologies to support and automate various aspects of an organization's information technology infrastructure. Software IT is used in a wide range of applications, including software development, network management, system administration, database management, and project management.

Software IT encompasses a variety of technologies and software applications, including:

1. **Programming languages and development frameworks:** These are used to build software applications and systems, and include languages

such as Java, Python, and JavaScript, as well as frameworks such as Angular, React, and Vue.js.

2. **DevOps tools:** These are used to automate and streamline software development, deployment, and operations, and include tools such as Jenkins, Ansible, and Docker.

3. **Cloud computing platforms:** These are used to host and manage applications and data in the cloud, and include platforms such as Amazon Web Services (AWS), Microsoft Azure, and Google Cloud Platform.

4. **Network management tools:** These are used to monitor and manage network infrastructure, and include tools such as Wireshark, Nagios, and SolarWinds.

5. **System administration tools:** These are used to manage and monitor operating systems and system infrastructure, and include tools such as Puppet, Chef, and Ansible.

6. **Database management tools:** These are used to manage and manipulate data stored in databases, and include tools such as MySQL, Oracle, and Microsoft SQL Server.

7. **Project management tools:** These are used to manage and track project activities and progress, and include tools such as JIRA, Trello, and Asana.

In addition to the tools and technologies mentioned earlier, Software IT also encompasses other related practices and methodologies that help organizations deliver high-quality software products and services. Some of these include:

1. **Agile software development:** Agile is a methodology that emphasizes collaboration, flexibility, and rapid iteration to deliver software products and services that better meet the needs of end-users. Agile development methods include Scrum, Kanban, and Lean.

2. **DevSecOps:** DevSecOps is an approach to software development that emphasizes security and compliance throughout the software development lifecycle. DevSecOps integrates security and compliance practices into the software development process, enabling organizations to deliver more secure and compliant software products and services.

3. **Continuous integration and continuous delivery (CI/CD):** CI/CD is a set of practices that enable organizations to deliver software products and services more quickly and with greater reliability. CI/CD involves automating the building, testing, and deployment of software applications, allowing organizations to quickly and reliably release new features and updates.

4. **Quality assurance and testing:** Quality assurance and testing are important practices that help organizations ensure that software

products and services meet high standards of quality and reliability. Quality assurance and testing practices include manual and automated testing, performance testing, and user acceptance testing.

Furthermore, as software becomes more critical to business operations, organizations are increasingly turning to Software IT to help them manage their software applications and infrastructure. Some benefits of using Software IT include:

1. **Increased Efficiency:** Software IT can automate and optimize IT-related tasks and processes, reducing the time and effort required to manage software applications and infrastructure.

2. **Improved Reliability:** Software IT can help organizations ensure that their software applications and infrastructure are reliable and available, improving uptime and minimizing downtime.

3. **Enhanced Security:** Software IT can help organizations manage and monitor their software applications and infrastructure for potential security threats, enabling them to quickly identify and remediate vulnerabilities.

4. **Better Collaboration:** Software IT can improve collaboration between different teams and

departments, enabling more effective communication and knowledge-sharing.

5. **Faster Time-to-Market:** Software IT can enable organizations to develop and deliver software products and services more quickly, enabling them to respond more quickly to changing market conditions and customer needs.

Moreover, the adoption of Software IT is not limited to large organizations and can be implemented by small and mid-sized businesses. Some key considerations that organizations should keep in mind when adopting Software IT include:

1. **Evaluate business needs:** Organizations should evaluate their business needs and determine which Software IT tools and practices are best suited to their specific requirements.

2. Choose the right tools and technologies: Organizations should choose the right tools and technologies that align with their business needs and budget.

3. **Training and education:** Organizations should invest in training and educating their staff on the tools and technologies they plan to use, to ensure they can use them effectively.

4. **Data management:** Organizations should develop data management practices that enable them to effectively manage and secure

their data, while also ensuring compliance with relevant regulations.

5. **Continuous improvement:** Organizations should continuously evaluate and improve their Software IT practices, to ensure they are delivering the best value and benefit to the organization.

In conclusion, Software IT is a critical component of modern IT management, enabling organizations to automate and optimize IT-related tasks and processes, reduce costs, improve collaboration, enhance security, and deliver high-quality software products and services more quickly and with greater reliability. By following the key considerations outlined earlier, organizations can successfully adopt Software IT and realize the benefits it provides, regardless of their size or industry.

## Software Legalities

Software legalities refer to the various legal issues that organizations must consider when developing, distributing, and using software. Some of the key legalities of software include:

1. **Intellectual property rights:** Software is protected by various forms of intellectual property rights, such as copyright, trademarks, patents, and trade secrets. Organizations must ensure that their software is protected and that

they respect the intellectual property rights of others.

2. **Licensing:** Software is licensed under various terms and conditions, such as proprietary licenses, open-source licenses, and copyleft licenses. Organizations must ensure that they comply with the licensing terms of the software they use and that they license their own software appropriately.

3. **Compliance:** Software must comply with various regulations and standards, such as data protection laws, export control regulations, and industry-specific standards. Organizations must ensure that their software is compliant with all relevant regulations and standards.

4. **Liability:** Organizations may be held liable for damages resulting from the use of their software, such as software defects, security breaches, and other issues. Organizations must take appropriate measures to minimize the risk of software-related damages and ensure that they have appropriate liability insurance.

5. **Contractual agreements:** Software is often subject to contractual agreements, such as end-user license agreements (EULAs) and service level agreements (SLAs). Organizations must ensure that they understand and comply with the terms of these agreements.

It is also important to note that software legalities can vary by country or region, as different jurisdictions have different laws and regulations related to software. Organizations that develop or distribute software in multiple countries or regions must be aware of the legal requirements in each of those jurisdictions and ensure that their software is compliant with all relevant laws and regulations.

Furthermore, as software becomes more complex and pervasive, new legal issues may arise. For example, the use of artificial intelligence and machine learning in software development and use can raise ethical and legal issues related to bias, privacy, and liability. Organizations must be aware of these emerging issues and take appropriate measures to address them.

To address the legal complexities of software, organizations may work with legal professionals or firms that specialize in software law. These professionals can provide guidance on legal compliance, intellectual property protection, and risk management, among other services.

Moreover, software legalities can also affect the business and financial aspects of software development and distribution. For example, licensing agreements can affect revenue models and profitability, while compliance issues can result in fines and legal liabilities that can negatively impact a company's finances.

In addition, the legalities of software can also impact an organization's reputation and brand. Legal issues related to software, such as security breaches or intellectual property disputes, can damage the trust and confidence that customers have in the organization.

To mitigate the financial and reputational risks associated with software legalities, organizations should take a proactive approach to legal compliance and risk management. This can include conducting regular legal reviews of software products and services, ensuring that all licenses and agreements are up-to-date and properly documented, and implementing robust data security and privacy practices.

Furthermore, organizations should prioritize transparency and communication with customers and other stakeholders regarding software legalities. This can help to build trust and confidence in the organization and its software products and services.

It's also worth noting that organizations must be aware of the legalities surrounding software in the context of emerging technologies and trends. For example, the rise of the Internet of Things (IoT) and connected devices has introduced new legal issues related to data privacy, cybersecurity, and liability.

Organizations that develop and distribute software for IoT devices must ensure that their software is secure and that they comply with data protection laws and regulations. They must also ensure that they have appropriate liability insurance and that they understand the legal implications of the data collected by their software.

Similarly, the use of blockchain technology in software development has introduced new legal issues related to intellectual property rights, data privacy, and compliance. Organizations that use blockchain technology in their software must understand the legal implications of the technology and ensure that they comply with all relevant laws and regulations.

In addition, the legalities of software are also impacted by the changing nature of software development itself. The adoption of agile development practices, the use of open-source software, and the increasing reliance on cloud-based software services have all introduced new legal issues related to intellectual property rights, licensing, and liability.

In conclusion, organizations must be aware of the legal complexities of software in the context of emerging technologies and trends. By understanding the legal implications of these technologies and taking a proactive approach to legal compliance and risk management, organizations can develop and distribute software products and services that are secure, compliant, and legally sound.

## S.A.M Cross-functional Collaboration

Software Asset Management (S.A.M) requires cross-functional collaboration across various departments within an organization. Effective collaboration ensures that S.A.M is integrated into the organization's overall strategy, and that S.A.M policies and procedures are followed consistently across all departments.

Some of the key departments and stakeholders involved in S.A.M cross-functional collaboration include:

1. **IT:** IT plays a critical role in S.A.M, as it is responsible for implementing and managing the software used by the organization. IT teams must work closely with the S.A.M team to ensure that software licenses are properly managed, software inventory is up-to-date, and software is being used in compliance with licensing agreements.

2. **Procurement:** Procurement teams are responsible for purchasing software licenses and managing vendor relationships. Procurement teams must work closely with the S.A.M team to ensure that software purchases are in line with the organization's needs, and

that licenses are properly managed and renewed.

3. **Legal:** Legal teams are responsible for ensuring that the organization is in compliance with relevant laws and regulations related to software, such as data protection and intellectual property laws. Legal teams must work closely with the S.A.M team to ensure that S.A.M policies and procedures are in line with legal requirements.

4. **Finance:** Finance teams are responsible for managing the organization's finances, including the cost of software licenses and renewals. Finance teams must work closely with the S.A.M team to ensure that software costs are properly managed and that the organization is getting the best value for its software investments.

5. **Business units:** Business units are responsible for using software to carry out their day-to-day operations. Business units must work closely with the S.A.M team to ensure that software is being used in compliance with licensing agreements, and that licenses are properly managed and renewed.

In addition to these departments and stakeholders, S.A.M cross-functional collaboration may also involve external vendors and partners, such as software vendors and S.A.M consultants.

To facilitate effective cross-functional collaboration, organizations can implement various strategies and best practices, such as:

1. **Developing a S.A.M policy:** A S.A.M policy outlines the organization's S.A.M goals, roles and responsibilities, and procedures for software procurement, deployment, and retirement. By developing a S.A.M policy, organizations can ensure that all stakeholders are on the S.A.M page and working towards the S.A.M goals.

2. **Establishing a S.A.M team:** A S.A.M team is responsible for managing the organization's software assets and ensuring that S.A.M policies and procedures are followed. The S.A.M team should have representatives from IT, procurement, legal, finance, and other relevant departments.

3. **Conducting regular S.A.M reviews:** Regular S.A.M reviews can help to identify software assets that are underutilized, over-licensed, or non-compliant with licensing agreements. S.A.M reviews can also help to identify opportunities for cost savings and process improvements.

4. **Providing S.A.M training:** Providing S.A.M training to all stakeholders can help to ensure that everyone understands the importance of

S.A.M and the procedures for managing software assets.

5. **Implementing S.A.M tools:** S.A.M tools can help to automate various S.A.M tasks, such as software discovery, inventory management, and license tracking. S.A.M tools can also provide real-time data on software usage and licensing compliance.

6. **Encouraging open communication:** Open communication between departments and stakeholders is critical for effective S.A.M cross-functional collaboration. Departments should work together to identify and resolve any issues related to S.A.M, and to share best practices and lessons learned.

It is important to note that S.A.M cross-functional collaboration is not a one-time event, but an ongoing process. As software evolves and new technologies and trends emerge, S.A.M policies and procedures must be updated and stakeholders must be kept informed.

In addition, S.A.M cross-functional collaboration can help organizations to achieve other strategic goals, such as digital transformation and innovation. By working together, stakeholders can identify opportunities to leverage software assets to drive innovation and improve operational efficiency.

Furthermore, S.A.M cross-functional collaboration can also help organizations to mitigate legal and financial risks related to software. By working together, stakeholders can identify and address compliance issues, minimize software-related liabilities, and optimize software licensing costs.

Overall, effective S.A.M cross-functional collaboration is critical for ensuring that software assets are properly managed and that organizations are in compliance with legal requirements and getting the best value for their software investments. By implementing best practices and fostering open communication between departments and stakeholders, organizations can achieve their S.A.M goals and achieve greater success in their overall business objectives.

Another important aspect of S.A.M cross-functional collaboration is to align S.A.M with the organization's overall business objectives. This means understanding how software assets can help the organization achieve its goals and how S.A.M can contribute to those objectives.

For example, if the organization's goal is to reduce costs and increase efficiency, S.A.M can help by identifying underutilized software assets and finding opportunities to optimize licensing costs. If the organization's goal is to improve customer service, S.A.M can help by ensuring that the software used by customer service teams is up-to-date and properly licensed, which can lead to faster and more efficient service.

S.A.M can also help organizations to achieve compliance with regulatory requirements, such as data protection laws and industry-specific regulations. By working with legal, IT, and other stakeholders, S.A.M can help ensure that software is being used in compliance with relevant regulations, which can help avoid costly fines and penalties.

To align S.A.M with the organization's business objectives, it's important to involve key stakeholders in the S.A.M planning process. This means working with business units, senior management, and other stakeholders to understand their software needs and how S.A.M can help them achieve their goals. By involving stakeholders in the planning process, organizations can ensure that S.A.M policies and procedures are tailored to the organization's specific needs and that everyone is invested in the success of the S.A.M program.

In addition, it's important to regularly evaluate the effectiveness of the organization's S.A.M program and make adjustments as needed. This means monitoring software usage and license compliance, as well as soliciting feedback from stakeholders on how the S.A.M program can be improved. By regularly evaluating and adjusting the S.A.M program, organizations can ensure that it remains aligned with the organization's business objectives and continues to provide value.

In conclusion, aligning S.A.M with the organization's business objectives is critical for ensuring that software assets are properly managed and that S.A.M policies and procedures are effective. By involving key stakeholders in the planning process, regularly evaluating the S.A.M program, and making adjustments as needed, organizations can ensure that S.A.M is contributing to the organization's overall success.

## S.A.M Business Alignment

Software Asset Management (S.A.M) is an important aspect of an organization's IT strategy, but it's also important to align S.A.M with the overall business strategy. By aligning S.A.M with the organization's business objectives, organizations can ensure that they are making the most of their software investments and contributing to the overall success of the organization.

To align S.A.M with the organization's business strategy, it's important to first understand the organization's goals and objectives. This means working closely with senior management and other key stakeholders to understand the organization's priorities and how software assets can help achieve those priorities. For example, if the organization's goal is to improve customer service, S.A.M can help by ensuring that the software used by customer service teams is up-to-date and properly licensed, which can lead to faster and more efficient service.

Once the organization's goals and priorities are understood, S.A.M policies and procedures can be tailored to support those goals. For example, if the organization's goal is to reduce costs, S.A.M can help by identifying underutilized software assets and finding opportunities to optimize licensing costs. If the organization's goal is to improve productivity, S.A.M can help by ensuring that software is up-to-date and properly licensed, which can help avoid downtime and other productivity issues.

In addition to tailoring S.A.M policies and procedures to support the organization's goals, it's also important to regularly evaluate the effectiveness of the S.A.M program and make adjustments as needed. This means monitoring software usage and license compliance, as well as soliciting feedback from stakeholders on how the S.A.M program can be improved. By regularly evaluating and adjusting the S.A.M program, organizations can ensure that it remains aligned with the organization's business objectives and continues to provide value.

Another important aspect of aligning S.A.M with the organization's business strategy is to ensure that all stakeholders are on the S.A.M page and working towards the S.A.M goals. This means communicating S.A.M policies and procedures to all relevant stakeholders and ensuring that everyone understands how S.A.M supports the organization's business objectives.

To communicate S.A.M policies and procedures effectively, it's important to use clear, concise language and to provide training and resources to all stakeholders. This means developing training materials, such as user guides and training videos, and providing regular updates on S.A.M policies and procedures to all relevant departments and stakeholders.

It's also important to encourage open communication between departments and stakeholders to ensure that everyone is informed and aligned around S.A.M policies and procedures. This means establishing regular communication channels, such as meetings and email updates, to provide a forum for stakeholders to share information and updates.

In addition, it's important to use metrics and data to track the effectiveness of the S.A.M program and to communicate that effectiveness to stakeholders. This means tracking software usage, license compliance, and cost savings, and sharing that information with relevant stakeholders to demonstrate the value of the S.A.M program.

Another important aspect of aligning S.A.M with the organization's business strategy is to ensure that S.A.M is integrated into the organization's overall governance framework. This means aligning S.A.M policies and procedures with other governance frameworks, such as IT governance, risk management, and compliance frameworks, to ensure that all aspects of the organization's governance are working together effectively.

By aligning S.A.M with other governance frameworks, organizations can avoid duplication of effort and ensure that all stakeholders are working together effectively to achieve the organization's goals. For example, if the organization has an IT governance framework in place, S.A.M policies and procedures can be integrated into that framework to ensure that software assets are being managed in compliance with the organization's overall IT strategy.

In addition, by aligning S.A.M with other governance frameworks, organizations can ensure that they are taking a holistic approach to managing risk and compliance. For example, by integrating S.A.M into the organization's overall risk management framework, the organization can ensure that software-related risks are being identified and managed effectively, which can help avoid costly compliance issues and other risks.

Finally, to align S.A.M with the organization's business strategy, it's important to regularly review and update S.A.M policies and procedures to ensure that they remain aligned with the organization's goals and priorities. This means regularly assessing the effectiveness of the S.A.M program, identifying areas for improvement, and making adjustments as needed.

Regular reviews of the S.A.M program can help ensure that it continues to provide value and that it remains aligned with the organization's goals and priorities. This means assessing the effectiveness of S.A.M policies and procedures, identifying areas where improvements can be made, and making changes as needed to ensure that the S.A.M program continues to support the organization's goals.

In addition to regular reviews of the S.A.M program, it's also important to keep up to date with changes in the software industry and to ensure that S.A.M policies and procedures are in line with industry best practices. This means keeping up to date with software licensing trends and changes, as well as regulatory changes that may affect S.A.M policies and procedures.

By regularly reviewing and updating S.A.M policies and procedures, organizations can ensure that they are taking a proactive approach to software asset management and that they are making the most of their software investments. This can help organizations to reduce costs, improve productivity, and avoid compliance issues, all of which can contribute to the overall success of the organization.

Overall, aligning S.A.M with the organization's business strategy requires a coordinated effort between IT, procurement, legal, finance, business units, and other stakeholders. By regularly reviewing and updating S.A.M policies and procedures, keeping up to date with changes in the software industry and aligning S.A.M with the organization's overall governance framework, organizations can ensure that they are making the most of their software investments and contributing to the overall success of the organization.

## Software Usage Monitoring

Software Usage Monitoring is a key component of Software Asset Management (S.A.M) that involves the continuous tracking and monitoring of the usage of software applications across an organization. This involves capturing data on how software is being used, by whom, and on which devices. This information can then be used to optimize licensing and reduce costs by identifying underutilized licenses, and to identify potential compliance issues by detecting unauthorized or unlicensed software.

Software usage monitoring can be achieved through the use of various tools and techniques such as software metering, license utilization analysis, and usage analytics. These tools provide insights into software usage patterns and trends, allowing organizations to make informed decisions about software licensing and usage.

Overall, software usage monitoring is critical for maintaining compliance, optimizing costs, and maximizing the value of an organization's software assets.

By monitoring software usage, organizations can gain visibility into the following:

1. **License Compliance:** Monitoring software usage helps to ensure that the organization is in compliance with software licensing agreements, and that the organization is only using licensed software.

2. **License Optimization:** By analyzing software usage data, organizations can identify opportunities to optimize license usage and reduce costs. For example, if a particular software application is not being used frequently, the organization may be able to reduce the number of licenses required.

3. **Software Procurement:** Usage data can also be used to inform software procurement decisions, by providing insight into which applications are being used and by whom.

4. **Security:** Monitoring software usage can help to identify potential security risks, such as the use of unapproved software or unauthorized access to software applications.

To effectively monitor software usage, organizations can use a variety of tools and techniques, including:

1. **Software Metering:** Software metering tools track the usage of software applications in real-time, providing insights into how software is being used.
2. **License Utilization Analysis:** By analyzing software usage data, organizations can gain insights into which licenses are being used most frequently and which licenses are underutilized. This information can be used to optimize licensing and reduce costs.
3. **Usage Analytics:** Usage analytics tools provide detailed insights into how software applications are being used, including which features are being used most frequently and by whom.
4. **User Behavior Analysis:** User behavior analysis tools can be used to identify anomalous behavior and potential security risks, such as the use of unapproved software or unauthorized access to software applications.

Overall, effective software usage monitoring requires a combination of tools and techniques, as well as a comprehensive S.A.M strategy that is aligned with the organization's business goals and objectives. By monitoring software usage effectively, organizations can gain a deeper understanding of how their software assets are being used, and use this information to optimize licensing, reduce costs, and maintain compliance.

In addition to tools and techniques, effective software usage monitoring also requires the cooperation and collaboration of all stakeholders within the organization. This includes IT teams, software vendors, procurement teams, and end-users.

To ensure effective collaboration, it is important to establish clear roles and responsibilities, and to communicate the importance of S.A.M and software usage monitoring across the organization. This can be achieved through training programs, workshops, and awareness campaigns.

In addition, organizations can establish processes and procedures for managing software assets throughout their lifecycle, including procurement, deployment, and disposal. This can help to ensure that software is being used effectively and efficiently, and that licensing is being optimized to reduce costs.

In conclusion, software usage monitoring is a critical component of S.A.M, and requires the cooperation and collaboration of all stakeholders to be effective. By monitoring software usage effectively, organizations can optimize licensing, reduce costs, maintain compliance, and maximize the value of their software assets.

## Cloud Software Management

Cloud software management is the process of managing software assets that are deployed in the cloud. With the rise of cloud computing, more and more software applications are being hosted in the cloud, and managing these assets can be challenging for organizations. Cloud software management involves tracking the deployment, usage, and cost of cloud-based software assets, as well as managing compliance with licensing agreements and regulations.

The cloud software management process typically includes the following steps:

1. **Software Inventory:** The first step in cloud software management is to conduct an inventory of all software applications that are deployed in the cloud. This can include both commercial software applications and internally developed applications.

2. **Usage Monitoring:** Once the software inventory is complete, the next step is to monitor usage of cloud-based software assets. This can include tracking the number of users, the frequency of use, and other usage metrics.

3. **License Management:** Cloud software management also involves managing licenses for cloud-based software assets. This can include monitoring license compliance, optimizing license usage, and negotiating licensing agreements with cloud service providers.

4. **Cost Management:** Cloud software management also involves managing the costs associated with cloud-based software assets. This can include monitoring usage costs, optimizing usage to reduce costs, and negotiating pricing agreements with cloud service providers.
5. **Compliance Management:** Finally, cloud software management involves managing compliance with licensing agreements and regulations. This can include tracking license usage, ensuring compliance with licensing terms and conditions, and managing software audits.

S.A.M tools can be used to track the deployment, usage, and cost of cloud-based software assets. These tools can help organizations to maintain an accurate inventory of cloud-based software assets, monitor usage and optimize license utilization, and manage compliance with licensing agreements and regulations. Some S.A.M tools also provide cost management features that help organizations to identify cost savings opportunities and negotiate pricing agreements with cloud service providers.

In addition to managing cloud-based software assets, cloud software management also involves managing relationships with cloud service providers. Cloud service providers often offer different pricing models and licensing terms than traditional software vendors, and it can be challenging to navigate these agreements. S.A.M tools can help organizations to negotiate better pricing agreements with cloud service providers and manage compliance with licensing terms and conditions.

S.A.M tools can provide organizations with a centralized view of their cloud-based software assets, enabling them to manage these assets more effectively. S.A.M tools can also provide usage tracking and license management features that help organizations to identify overused and underused software assets and optimize their license usage. S.A.M tools can also provide automated reports on license utilization and costs, enabling organizations to make data-driven decisions about their cloud software usage and procurement.

Cloud software management also involves managing compliance with licensing agreements and regulations. Many cloud-based software licenses have unique terms and conditions that must be tracked and managed to ensure compliance. S.A.M tools can help organizations to automate compliance management by providing automated alerts for license renewals, usage violations, and other compliance-related issues. S.A.M tools can also provide audit defense features, helping organizations to prepare for software audits and respond to audit requests quickly and accurately.

In addition to the benefits mentioned earlier, effective cloud software management can also help organizations to improve their security posture. Cloud-based software assets are often accessed from multiple locations and devices, making them more vulnerable to security breaches. By tracking software usage and ensuring that all software assets are up to date and patched, organizations can reduce the risk of security breaches and improve their overall security posture.

Furthermore, cloud software management can also help organizations to ensure that their software assets are being used effectively and efficiently. By tracking software usage, organizations can identify underutilized software assets and make informed decisions about which software assets to renew or discontinue. This can help organizations to optimize their software investments and reduce unnecessary costs.

Another important aspect of cloud software management is managing vendor relationships. Cloud service providers often have unique licensing terms and pricing models, and it can be challenging to manage these relationships effectively. S.A.M tools can help organizations to manage vendor relationships more effectively by providing automated alerts for licensing renewals and usage violations, negotiating better pricing agreements, and ensuring compliance with licensing terms and conditions.

Overall, cloud software management is a critical process for organizations that rely on cloud-based software to support their operations. Effective cloud software management can help organizations to improve their security posture, optimize their software investments, and manage vendor relationships more effectively. S.A.M tools can help to automate and streamline the cloud software management process, making it faster, more accurate, and more effective.

## Software Enterprise Agreements

A software enterprise agreement is a licensing agreement between a software vendor and an enterprise that provides the enterprise with a set of licenses for a specific set of software products. Enterprise agreements are typically designed for large organizations with a significant number of users or devices that require access to the software products.

An enterprise agreement typically provides the enterprise with a set of licenses that can be used across the organization, rather than having to purchase individual licenses for each user or device. This can provide cost savings for the enterprise and simplify software license management.

Enterprise agreements can include a variety of different licensing options, such as perpetual licenses, subscription licenses, and volume licenses. They can also include access to additional services or support, such as training and technical support.

Effective management of enterprise agreements is critical to ensuring that organizations are getting the most value out of their software investments. S.A.M tools can help organizations to track their software licenses, monitor usage, and manage compliance with licensing agreements and regulations. S.A.M tools can also help organizations to optimize their license usage and identify opportunities for cost savings by analyzing usage patterns and identifying underutilized software assets.

In summary, enterprise agreements provide organizations with a convenient and cost-effective way to manage their software licenses. By effectively managing their enterprise agreements and leveraging S.A.M tools to track and optimize their license usage, organizations can reduce costs, improve compliance, and get the most value out of their software investments.

## Service Level Agreements

A Service Level Agreement (SLA) is a contract between a service provider and a customer that defines the level of service that will be provided. SLAs are commonly used in the IT industry to establish service expectations for various IT services, including software support and maintenance.

In the context of Software Asset Management (S.A.M), SLAs can be used to define the level of support and maintenance that a software vendor will provide for their products. This can include technical support, software updates, and patches, and other maintenance activities.

An effective S.A.M program should include a process for managing SLAs with software vendors. This can include monitoring SLA compliance, tracking support requests and resolutions, and identifying opportunities for renegotiation or optimization of SLAs.

S.A.M tools can be used to manage SLAs by tracking support requests and monitoring compliance with SLA terms. S.A.M tools can also be used to identify areas where SLAs can be optimized, such as renegotiating support hours or adjusting response times.

Overall, effective management of SLAs is an important aspect of S.A.M. By establishing clear service expectations and monitoring compliance with SLA terms, organizations can ensure that they are receiving the level of service they need from their software vendors. S.A.M tools can be used to automate and streamline the SLA management process, making it faster, more accurate, and more effective.

Contract Management

Contract management is the process of managing the lifecycle of contracts, from creation and negotiation to execution and renewal. This involves a range of activities, such as contract drafting, review, negotiation, and approval, as well as ongoing monitoring and management of contract performance.

Effective contract management is important for organizations to ensure that they are meeting contractual obligations, managing risks, and maintaining good relationships with vendors and partners. It can also help organizations to identify opportunities to improve contract terms and reduce costs.

Some key elements of contract management include:

1. **Contract creation and negotiation:** This involves the development of contract terms and conditions, negotiation of terms with suppliers or customers, and finalization of the contract.
2. **Contract execution and monitoring:** This includes the monitoring of contract compliance and performance, as well as the management of any disputes or issues that arise during the contract term.
3. **Contract renewal and termination:** This involves the review and negotiation of new contract terms at the end of a contract term, as well as the termination of contracts that are no longer needed or are not meeting organizational requirements.

Contract management software can help organizations to streamline these processes, automate contract administration tasks, and improve contract compliance and performance. Some popular contract management tools include Agiloft, ContractWorks, and ContractSafe.

## Software Governance and Compliance.

Software governance and compliance refers to the process of establishing policies and procedures to ensure that software assets are managed in a way that is compliant with internal policies and external regulations. The primary goal of software governance and compliance is to minimize the risk of non-compliance and avoid costly fines and legal actions.

Here are some ways that S.A.M (Software Asset Management) can help with software governance and compliance:

1. **Software Inventory:** S.A.M can help create and maintain a comprehensive inventory of software installations and licenses, which can be used to ensure that all software usage is in compliance with internal policies and external regulations.
2. **License Tracking:** S.A.M tools can track all software licenses and ensure that an organization has the appropriate number of licenses for their software usage.

3. **Compliance Reporting:** S.A.M can generate compliance reports that show an organization's compliance status and identify any areas where it is not in compliance. This can help organizations avoid non-compliance and costly fines associated with non-compliance.
4. **Contract Management:** S.A.M can help manage software contracts and ensure that they are in compliance with all applicable laws and regulations.
5. **Software Usage Monitoring:** S.A.M can monitor software usage patterns to identify any potential compliance risks and take corrective action.
6. **IT Governance:** S.A.M can be integrated with IT governance policies to ensure that all software usage is in line with internal policies and external regulations.

By using S.A.M to manage software assets and ensure compliance, organizations can reduce the risk of non-compliance, avoid costly fines and legal actions, and maintain a good reputation. This can result in significant cost savings over time and help organizations better manage their overall software investments.

S.A.M can also help organizations maintain compliance with licensing terms and conditions. This includes ensuring that software is only being used by authorized users and that the software is not being used in a way that violates the licensing agreement. S.A.M can also help manage software licenses and ensure that the organization is not over- or under-licensed, which can lead to compliance issues.

S.A.M can also help organizations maintain compliance with regulations related to data privacy and security. By ensuring that software is properly licensed and configured, S.A.M can help protect sensitive data from unauthorized access or misuse. This can help organizations avoid data breaches and the legal and financial consequences that come with them.

S.A.M can also help organizations maintain compliance with open source licenses. By identifying open source software and tracking its usage, S.A.M can help organizations ensure that they are in compliance with the terms of the open source license.

Overall, software governance and compliance are an essential component of any organization's software asset management strategy. By establishing policies and procedures that promote compliance, and by using S.A.M to manage software assets, organizations can minimize the risk of non-compliance and avoid costly fines and legal actions.

In addition to the benefits of reducing risk and avoiding non-compliance, software governance and compliance can also help organizations optimize their software investments. By tracking software usage and license compliance, organizations can identify opportunities to consolidate or eliminate licenses, reduce costs, and optimize software utilization. This can result in significant cost savings and better management of software investments.

To achieve the benefits of software governance and compliance, organizations need to establish a culture of compliance that emphasizes the importance of managing software assets in a way that is compliant with internal policies and external regulations. This requires buy-in from all levels of the organization, from senior management to individual users, and a commitment to ongoing training and education.

S.A.M can help organizations establish and maintain a culture of compliance by providing tools and processes that support compliance with software license terms and conditions, internal policies, and external regulations. By leveraging S.A.M, organizations can ensure that their software assets are managed in a way that supports both compliance and cost optimization, while minimizing risk and avoiding costly fines and legal actions.

## S.A.M Compliance Reporting

S.A.M (Software Asset Management) compliance reporting is an important function that helps organizations maintain compliance with software license agreements and avoid costly fines and penalties associated with non-compliance. Compliance reporting involves generating reports that show an organization's compliance status and identifying any areas where it is not in compliance.

Here are some ways that S.A.M can help with compliance reporting:

1. **License Tracking:** S.A.M tools can track all software licenses and ensure that an organization has the appropriate number of licenses for their software usage.

2. **License Optimization:** S.A.M can help optimize software licenses to ensure that organizations are in compliance with licensing agreements, and avoid overuse of licenses.

3. **License Reconciliation:** S.A.M can help reconcile software license usage with licenses to ensure compliance and avoid the overuse of licenses.

4. **License Metrics:** S.A.M can help understand software license metrics and ensure that licenses are assigned correctly, such as user-based or device-based licenses.

5. **Data Analysis:** S.A.M can provide data analysis tools to help identify compliance risks, such as software usage patterns, license overuse, and non-compliant installations.

6. **Compliance Reporting:** S.A.M can generate compliance reports that show an organization's compliance status and identify any areas where

it is not in compliance. This can help organizations avoid non-compliance and costly fines associated with non-compliance.

By using S.A.M to manage software licenses and generate compliance reports, organizations can better understand their software license compliance status and take action to maintain compliance. This can result in significant cost savings over time and help organizations better manage their overall software investments.

## Data Privacy Compliance

Data privacy compliance is the practice of ensuring that personal data is collected, processed, stored, and shared in accordance with applicable laws and regulations. This includes laws such as the EU General Data Protection Regulation (GDPR), the California Consumer Privacy Act (CCPA), and others.

To ensure data privacy compliance, organizations should consider the following best practices:

1. **Conduct a Data Inventory:** Identify all software applications and devices that collect, use, or store personal data.
2. **Develop a Privacy Policy:** Develop a formal privacy policy that outlines the organization's data privacy practices and obligations under applicable laws.

3. **Conduct a privacy impact assessment:** Conduct a privacy impact assessment to identify and address potential privacy risks associated with the collection, use, and storage of personal data.
4. **Implement technical and organizational measures:** Implement technical and organizational measures to ensure the security and confidentiality of personal data, including access controls, encryption, and data backups.
5. **Maintain documentation:** Maintain detailed documentation of data privacy practices and procedures, including data inventories, privacy policies, and privacy impact assessments.
6. **Monitor compliance:** Regularly monitor compliance with applicable data protection laws and regulations and make necessary adjustments to software and processes to ensure ongoing compliance.
7. **Provide employee training:** Provide employee training on data privacy laws and regulations, as well as the organization's data privacy practices and procedures.
8. **Maintain an incident response plan:** Develop and maintain an incident response plan to respond quickly and effectively to data breaches and other privacy incidents.
9. **Conduct regular audits:** Conduct regular audits of software and data privacy practices to ensure

ongoing compliance with applicable laws and regulations.

10. **Stay informed about changes in data privacy laws:** Stay up-to-date with changes in data privacy laws and regulations and adjust software and processes accordingly.

By implementing these best practices, organizations can ensure that personal data is collected, used, and stored in accordance with applicable data protection laws and regulations. This can help to minimize the risk of data breaches and regulatory fines, as well as protect the privacy rights of individuals.

In addition to these best practices, organizations can also benefit from the use of software tools and services that help to automate data privacy compliance tasks, such as data inventory and management, consent management, and data subject requests.

Examples of software tools for data privacy compliance include:

1. **Data inventory and mapping tools:** Tools that help organizations identify, classify, and map personal data across their software applications and devices.

2. **Consent management tools:** Tools that enable organizations to obtain and manage user consent for the collection, use, and sharing of personal data.

3. **Data subject request management tools:** Tools that help organizations manage data subject requests, such as access requests, rectification requests, and erasure requests.

4. **Data protection impact assessment (DPIA) tools:** Tools that help organizations conduct privacy impact assessments in accordance with applicable data protection laws and regulations.

5. **Privacy management software:** Comprehensive software solutions that help organizations manage all aspects of data privacy compliance, including data inventory, privacy policies, consent management, data subject request management, and DPIAs.

By using these tools, organizations can automate many of the tasks associated with data privacy compliance, which can help to reduce the risk of human error and ensure consistent compliance with applicable laws and regulations.

Organizations can also benefit from implementing best practices for data privacy compliance, including:

1. Conducting a privacy impact assessment (PIA) to identify and mitigate privacy risks associated with new projects or initiatives.

2. Implementing appropriate technical and organizational measures to ensure the security of personal data, such as access controls, encryption, and data backups.

3. Appointing a data protection officer (DPO) to oversee data privacy compliance and serve as a point of contact for data subjects and regulatory authorities.
4. Developing and implementing a comprehensive privacy policy that describes how personal data is collected, used, and shared by the organization.
5. Implementing a process for obtaining and managing user consent for the collection, use, and sharing of personal data.
6. Establishing a process for managing data subject requests, such as access requests, rectification requests, and erasure requests.
7. Providing training and awareness programs for employees on data privacy best practices and regulatory requirements.
8. Regularly reviewing and updating data privacy policies and practices to ensure compliance with changing regulatory requirements.

By implementing these best practices and using appropriate software tools and services, organizations can effectively manage data privacy compliance and ensure the protection of personal data.

## Data Inventory and Mapping Tools

Data inventory and mapping tools are software applications that help organizations identify and manage the personal data they collect, process, and store. These tools can automate the data discovery process, providing a more comprehensive view of the organization's data assets, and facilitate compliance with data privacy regulations.

Some examples of data inventory and mapping tools include:

1. **OneTrust:** a comprehensive privacy management platform that includes data inventory and mapping capabilities.
2. **DataGrail:** a platform that automates data subject requests, provides real-time visibility into data usage, and maps data across the organization.
3. **BigID:** a privacy management platform that uses machine learning to identify personal data, manage data retention, and map data flows.
4. **Collibra:** a data intelligence platform that includes data inventory and mapping features as part of its data governance capabilities.
5. **Informatica:** a data integration and management platform that includes a data catalog with inventory and mapping capabilities.

By using these tools, organizations can more effectively manage their data assets, assess privacy risks, and ensure compliance with data privacy regulations.

## Cost Management for Cloud Services

Software Asset Management (S.A.M) can help organizations effectively manage costs for cloud services by optimizing their usage and ensuring compliance with licensing agreements.

Here are some ways that S.A.M can help with cost management for cloud services:

1. **Usage Monitoring:** S.A.M tools can monitor cloud service usage to identify underutilized resources and to determine if usage is in line with licensing agreements.
2. **License Optimization:** S.A.M tools can help organizations optimize cloud service licensing by identifying areas where licenses can be reduced or consolidated, such as identifying unused or underutilized licenses.
3. **License Reconciliation:** S.A.M can help organizations reconcile cloud service usage with licenses to ensure compliance and avoid unnecessary expenses, such as the overuse of cloud services.
4. **Contract Management:** S.A.M can help organizations manage their cloud service contracts to ensure that they are getting the best pricing and that they are not paying for unnecessary services.
5. **Procurement Strategy:** S.A.M can help organizations identify the most cost-effective

procurement strategy for cloud services, such as buying in bulk or negotiating volume discounts.

6. **Cloud Service Provider Management:** S.A.M can help organizations manage their relationships with cloud service providers to ensure they are getting the best service and pricing.

By using S.A.M to manage cloud services, organizations can identify areas where they can reduce costs, ensure compliance with licensing agreements, and optimize their cloud service usage. This can result in significant cost savings over time and help organizations better manage their overall software investments.

## Invoices

S.A.M (Software Asset Management) can help organizations manage invoices related to software licenses by providing a centralized view of all software license agreements, their terms and conditions, and associated costs. Here are some ways that S.A.M can help with managing software license invoices:

1. **License Tracking:** S.A.M tools can track software license agreements and track their costs, which can help organizations understand how much they are spending on software licenses and when payments are due.

2. **Invoice Management:** S.A.M tools can help organizations manage invoices related to software licenses, such as tracking invoice due

dates, managing payment schedules, and reconciling invoices against license usage.

3. **Contract Management:** S.A.M can help organizations manage their software license contracts to ensure that they are getting the best pricing and that they are not paying for unnecessary software licenses.

4. **Usage Monitoring:** S.A.M can monitor software license usage to ensure that organizations are not overpaying for licenses that are not being used.

5. **Compliance Reporting:** S.A.M can generate reports on license compliance, which can help organizations avoid costly fines and penalties for non-compliance.

6. **Cost Allocation:** S.A.M can help organizations allocate software license costs to the appropriate departments, business units, or projects, which can help with budgeting and cost management.

By using S.A.M to manage software license invoices, organizations can ensure that they are paying for only the software licenses they need, and that they are paying the best possible price. S.A.M can also help organizations avoid non-compliance and costly fines associated with non-compliance, while ensuring that invoices are managed efficiently and effectively.

## Software Data Analysis

Software data analysis refers to the process of analyzing data related to software usage, licenses, and other related metrics to gain insights and make informed decisions. Data analysis in software asset management (S.A.M) can help organizations to optimize their software usage and licenses, reduce costs, and ensure compliance with software license agreements.

Here are some ways that S.A.M can help with software data analysis:

1. **Software Inventory:** S.A.M tools can help create and maintain a comprehensive inventory of software installations and licenses, which can be used to analyze software usage patterns.

2. **License Tracking:** S.A.M tools can track all software licenses and ensure that an organization has the appropriate number of licenses for their software usage. This data can be analyzed to identify areas where licenses can be optimized or consolidated.

3. **Usage Tracking:** S.A.M tools can track software usage patterns to identify underutilized or unused software, which can help optimize license usage and reduce costs.

4. **Compliance Reporting:** S.A.M can generate compliance reports that show an organization's compliance status and identify any areas where

it is not in compliance. This data can be analyzed to identify compliance risks and take action to maintain compliance.

5. **Data Visualization:** S.A.M tools can use data visualization techniques to present data in a way that is easy to understand and identify trends, patterns, and outliers.

6. **Predictive Analysis:** S.A.M can use predictive analysis to forecast software usage patterns and identify potential compliance risks or license optimization opportunities.

By using S.A.M to manage software licenses and analyze software usage data, organizations can make informed decisions to optimize license usage, reduce costs, and maintain compliance with software license agreements. This can result in significant cost savings over time and help organizations better manage their overall software investments.

## Cost Analysis Comparison

Cost analysis comparison is the process of comparing the costs associated with different software licensing models, procurement strategies, and vendor agreements to identify the most cost-effective approach for an organization.

Cost analysis comparison cost analysis comparison typically involves analyzing data from various sources, such as software inventory and usage data, licensing entitlements, vendor agreements, and procurement data. This data can be used to model different licensing scenarios and procurement strategies, and to estimate the total cost of ownership (TCO) for each approach.

S.A.M tools can be used to automate cost analysis comparison by providing real-time data on software usage and licensing, and by allowing organizations to model different licensing scenarios and procurement strategies. S.A.M tools can also provide visualizations and reports that help organizations to understand the cost implications of different licensing and procurement approaches.

Effective cost analysis comparison can help organizations to optimize their software investments by identifying the most cost-effective licensing models and procurement strategies. By using S.A.M tools to automate and streamline the cost analysis comparison process, organizations can save time, reduce costs, and make informed decisions about their software assets.

In summary, cost analysis comparison is an important aspect of S.A.M that can help organizations to optimize their software investments and reduce costs. S.A.M tools can be used to automate and streamline the cost analysis comparison process, providing real-time insights and helping organizations to make informed decisions about their software assets.

## Software Asset Disposal

Software asset disposal is an important component of any software asset management strategy. It involves removing software and data from devices that are no longer in use, and ensuring that sensitive data is securely and permanently erased to prevent unauthorized access.

Software asset disposal typically involves several steps. First, software assets need to be identified and cataloged. This includes identifying all software applications, data files, and user data associated with the device. Once the assets have been identified, they can be removed from the device and the data can be erased.

The data erasure process typically involves using specialized software tools to overwrite data on the device, making it unrecoverable. This is important to prevent data breaches and protect sensitive information from unauthorized access. Once the data has been securely erased, the device can be disposed of or repurposed.

In addition to data erasure, software asset disposal also involves ensuring that software licenses associated with the device are properly deactivated or transferred to other devices. This helps to prevent over- or under-licensing, which can lead to compliance issues.

It's important to note that software asset disposal should be considered throughout the software asset lifecycle, rather than as an afterthought. For example, during the procurement stage, organizations should consider how they will dispose of the software and associated data at the end of its lifecycle. This can help to ensure that the software is purchased with the right end-of-life plan in mind.

Similarly, during the deployment and installation stage, organizations should consider how software will be uninstalled and data will be erased when it is no longer needed. This can help to minimize the amount of sensitive data that is left on devices that are no longer in use.

Finally, during the ongoing management stage, organizations should regularly review their software asset inventory to identify devices that are no longer in use and can be disposed of. This can help to ensure that the organization is not over-licensing or wasting money on unnecessary software licenses.

To implement an effective software asset disposal strategy, organizations should consider the following best practices:

1. **Develop a Policy:** Create a formal policy for software asset disposal that outlines the process for identifying, cataloging, and securely erasing software assets and associated data.

2. **Identify Assets:** Identify all software assets, including applications, data files, and user data associated with devices that are no longer in use.
3. **Erase Data:** Erase data using specialized software tools to overwrite it, making it unrecoverable.
4. **Deactivate or Transfer Licenses:** Deactivate or transfer software licenses associated with the device to prevent over- or under-licensing.
5. **Dispose of Hardware:** Dispose of hardware in an environmentally responsible way, following best practices for electronic waste disposal.
6. **Maintain Documentation:** Maintain detailed documentation of the disposal process, including when and how software and data were erased and licenses were deactivated or transferred.
7. **Review and Update Regularly:** Review and update the software asset disposal policy and process on a regular basis to ensure it remains effective and aligned with organizational goals.

By following these best practices, organizations can ensure that software assets and associated data are disposed of in a secure and compliant manner. This can help to reduce the risk of data breaches and compliance issues, and optimize software investments.

In addition to these best practices, it is important to consider legal and regulatory requirements when disposing of software assets. For example, many countries have data protection laws that require organizations to ensure that personal data is securely erased when it is no longer needed.

In addition to legal and regulatory compliance, organizations should also consider the potential environmental impact of software asset disposal. This includes properly disposing of hardware in an environmentally responsible way and minimizing the amount of electronic waste generated by software asset disposal.

To minimize the environmental impact of software asset disposal, organizations can consider implementing a program to refurbish, repurpose, or donate devices that are still functional. Alternatively, they can work with specialized electronic waste disposal services that can safely dispose of hardware while minimizing the amount of waste generated.

Overall, software asset disposal is an important component of software asset management that requires careful planning and execution. By following best practices and considering legal, regulatory, and environmental requirements, organizations can ensure that software assets and associated data are disposed of in a secure and compliant manner.

In addition to these tools and resources, Microsoft also provides guidance and best practices for software asset management, including guidance on license compliance, license optimization, and software usage monitoring. By leveraging these tools and resources, organizations can improve their management of software assets, reduce compliance risks, and optimize their software spend.

## The Software Asset Manager

The Software Asset Manager (SAM) is a role responsible for managing an organization's software assets and ensuring compliance with software licensing agreements. The SAM is typically responsible for the following tasks:

1. **Software inventory management:** The SAM is responsible for creating and maintaining an accurate inventory of all software assets within the organization, including licenses, usage, and costs.

2. **License compliance management:** The SAM is responsible for ensuring compliance with all software licensing agreements, including tracking licenses, identifying any license overuse, and managing software audits.

3. **Software procurement management:** The SAM is responsible for managing the procurement of new software assets, ensuring that all new software purchases are compliant with

licensing agreements and aligned with the organization's needs.

4. **Software usage management:** The SAM is responsible for tracking software usage across the organization, identifying any underutilization or overutilization of software assets, and taking steps to optimize usage and reduce costs.

5. **Reporting and analytics:** The SAM is responsible for providing reports and analytics on software usage, compliance, and costs, to support decision-making and ensure that the organization is getting the most value from its software assets.

6. **Vendor management:** The SAM is responsible for managing relationships with software vendors, negotiating contracts, and ensuring that vendors are meeting their contractual obligations.

The SAM plays a critical role in ensuring that an organization is managing its software assets effectively, and in compliance with licensing agreements and regulatory requirements. By optimizing software usage and reducing costs associated with over-licensing and under-licensing, the SAM can help organizations to save costs, improve compliance, and make better decisions about software investments.

## The Scope of Software

The scope of software refers to the extent of the activities that can be carried out through software. In general, software can be designed to perform a wide range of tasks, from simple functions to complex applications.

At its most basic level, software can be used to perform tasks such as word processing, data entry, and basic calculations. As the complexity of the software increases, it can be used to perform more advanced tasks, such as running complex simulations, managing large databases, or automating complex business processes.

Some of the most common types of software include operating systems, productivity tools, graphics and design software, gaming software, and specialized applications for industries such as healthcare, finance, and engineering.

The scope of software is constantly expanding, as advances in technology enable developers to create more sophisticated applications that can perform increasingly complex tasks. As a result, the potential uses for software are virtually limitless, and the scope of software will continue to expand as technology continues to evolve.

## Strategic License Management

Strategic license management refers to the process of managing software licenses in a way that supports an organization's broader strategic goals. This involves not only ensuring compliance with licensing agreements, but also optimizing the use of software licenses to achieve maximum value for the organization.

Effective strategic license management can help organizations reduce costs, minimize legal and financial risks, and improve operational efficiency. This involves several key steps, including:

1. **Understanding licensing agreements:** Organizations need to have a clear understanding of the licensing agreements for the software they use, including the terms of use, limitations, and renewal requirements.
2. **Managing licenses:** Organizations need to have a centralized system for managing their software licenses, including tracking license usage, expiration dates, and renewals.
3. **Optimizing license usage:** Organizations need to ensure that their software licenses are being used efficiently and effectively, including avoiding over-licensing and under-licensing.
4. **Negotiating with vendors:** Organizations need to have strong relationships with their software vendors and negotiate favorable licensing terms and pricing.

5.  **Continual evaluation:** Organizations need to
    continually evaluate their software usage and
    licensing needs to ensure they are aligned with
    their strategic goals and business needs.

Overall, strategic license management is an important
aspect of any organization's IT strategy, as it helps to
ensure compliance, reduce costs, and optimize the use
of technology resources.

Software Harvesting

Software harvesting is the process of extracting
reusable software components from existing software
systems, in order to use them in other applications.
This process involves analyzing the existing software
system, identifying software components that can be
reused, and then extracting those components and
making them available for use in other applications.

Software harvesting can help organizations reduce
software development costs and accelerate the
development of new applications by leveraging
existing software assets. By reusing software
components, developers can avoid the time-
consuming and costly process of developing new
software from scratch.

The process of software harvesting typically involves
several steps, including:

1.  Analyzing the existing software system to
    identify reusable components.

2. Extracting the identified components and creating a library of reusable components.
3. Documenting the components to make them easily accessible and understandable to other developers.
4. Testing the components to ensure they function as intended and are compatible with other systems.
5. Maintaining the component library over time, updating and refining it as new components are identified and added.

Software harvesting is most effective when applied to software systems that are modular and well-structured, with clearly defined interfaces and documentation. However, it can be challenging to identify and extract reusable components from legacy software systems that were not designed with software harvesting in mind. Nonetheless, software harvesting can be a valuable approach to software development, particularly in larger organizations with many software systems that share common functionality.

## License Documentation

License documentation refers to the records and information related to the software licenses that an organization holds. This documentation is important for ensuring compliance with software licensing agreements and for managing software assets effectively.

License documentation typically includes the following information:

1. **License agreements:** Copies of the actual software license agreements that have been signed with vendors or software providers. This includes information such as the terms and conditions of use, the number of licenses purchased, and the renewal requirements.
2. **License keys:** Documentation of the license keys or activation codes required to install and activate the software.
3. **License usage:** Records of how the software is being used within the organization, including information about the number of licenses in use, who is using them, and how frequently they are being used.
4. **License renewal schedules:** Information on when licenses are due to expire and when they need to be renewed.
5. **License compliance:** Records of any compliance issues or violations that have been identified, and any actions that have been taken to address these issues.

Having accurate and up-to-date license documentation is essential for ensuring compliance with software licensing agreements, avoiding legal and financial risks, and optimizing the use of software assets. Organizations that manage their software licenses effectively can reduce costs, improve operational efficiency, and make better-informed decisions about their technology investments.

There are various software asset management tools available that can help organizations manage their software licenses and documentation more effectively, by automating many of the tasks associated with tracking and managing software assets.

## Proactive vs. Reactive SAM

Software Asset Management (SAM) is the process of managing an organization's software assets, including licenses, contracts, and usage, in order to ensure compliance, optimize costs, and improve operational efficiency. SAM can be either proactive or reactive, depending on the approach taken by the organization.

Proactive SAM involves a strategic, forward-looking approach to managing software assets. This approach involves:

1. Regular monitoring and tracking of software licenses and usage to ensure compliance and identify potential compliance risks before they become issues.
2. Adoption of best practices for software asset management, including use of automated tools

and processes to track and manage software assets.

3. Continuous optimization of software assets to reduce costs, improve efficiencies, and align with business goals.

Proactive SAM helps organizations to stay ahead of compliance risks, optimize their software usage, and make informed decisions about their technology investments.

Reactive SAM, on the other hand, is a more ad hoc and reactive approach to managing software assets. This approach involves:

1. Addressing compliance issues and risks as they arise, rather than proactively monitoring and managing them.
2. Responding to software license audits, and making changes only when necessary to meet compliance requirements.
3. Ad-hoc management of software assets, rather than adopting a systematic, best-practice approach.

Reactive SAM can lead to increased costs, legal and financial risks, and inefficiencies in managing software assets.

In summary, while both proactive and reactive SAM approaches have their advantages, organizations that adopt a proactive approach to software asset management are more likely to reduce costs, improve compliance, and optimize their software usage over the long term.

## Developing Goals

Developing goals is an important process for individuals, teams, and organizations to set clear targets and objectives that align with their overall mission and vision. Here are some key steps to developing effective goals:

1. **Define your mission and vision:** Before setting goals, it's important to have a clear understanding of the overall mission and vision of the organization or team. This helps to ensure that goals are aligned with the organization's overall direction.

2. **Identify key performance indicators (KPIs):** Key performance indicators are the metrics used to measure progress toward goals. It's important to identify KPIs that are specific, measurable, attainable, relevant, and time-bound (SMART) for each goal.

3. **Determine the scope and timeline:** Set a realistic timeline for achieving each goal, and determine the scope of work required to achieve them. This includes identifying the resources needed, such as personnel, tools, and funding.

4. **Engage stakeholders:** Involve stakeholders in the goal-setting process to gain their input and support. This helps to ensure that goals are realistic, achievable, and aligned with the needs and expectations of all stakeholders.
5. **Establish a plan of action:** Develop a plan of action that outlines the steps required to achieve each goal, including timelines, resources, and accountability measures.
6. **Monitor progress:** Regularly monitor progress toward achieving each goal, and make adjustments as needed to stay on track.
7. **Celebrate successes:** Celebrate achievements and milestones along the way to keep motivation high and maintain momentum toward achieving the overall goals.

Effective goal-setting is a critical process for achieving success in any endeavor. By following these key steps, individuals, teams, and organizations can set clear, achievable goals that help them to focus their efforts and achieve their desired outcomes.

## Savings Opportunities

There are many savings opportunities that organizations can take advantage of to reduce costs and improve their bottom line. Here are some potential areas for savings:

1. **Software licensing:** Software licensing can be a significant expense for many organizations. By

proactively managing software licenses and usage, organizations can reduce costs and ensure compliance with licensing agreements.

2. **Cloud services:** Cloud services can offer significant cost savings for organizations by providing a flexible and scalable IT infrastructure that can be tailored to the organization's specific needs. Cloud services can also help reduce hardware and maintenance costs.

3. **Energy efficiency:** Implementing energy-efficient practices can reduce utility costs, such as through the use of energy-efficient lighting, equipment, and HVAC systems.

4. **Telecommunications:** By evaluating telecommunications services and providers, organizations can identify cost savings opportunities for internet, phone, and mobile services.

5. **Supply chain optimization:** By optimizing the supply chain, organizations can reduce costs and improve operational efficiency, such as by streamlining procurement processes, reducing inventory costs, and improving supplier management.

6. **Outsourcing:** Outsourcing certain functions or processes can help organizations reduce costs by leveraging external expertise and resources,

and avoiding the need to hire and manage additional staff.

7. **Employee productivity:** Improving employee productivity can have a direct impact on an organization's bottom line. This can be achieved through training and development programs, improving employee engagement and satisfaction, and implementing technologies that enable employees to work more efficiently.

By identifying and pursuing these and other savings opportunities, organizations can reduce costs and improve their bottom line, while maintaining or even enhancing their level of service and quality.

ITAM Compliance

ITAM compliance refers to the process of ensuring that an organization's software and hardware assets are in compliance with relevant laws and regulations, as well as with the organization's own policies and procedures. ITAM compliance is important for minimizing legal and financial risks, optimizing IT investments, and maintaining the overall security and reliability of the IT infrastructure.

To achieve ITAM compliance, organizations need to take the following steps:

1. **Identify the relevant laws and regulations:** ITAM compliance requires a clear

understanding of the relevant laws and regulations that govern software and hardware asset management in the organization's jurisdiction, such as data privacy laws and regulations related to software licensing.

2. **Develop policies and procedures:** Organizations need to develop clear policies and procedures for managing software and hardware assets that are in compliance with relevant laws and regulations.

3. **Implement tracking and reporting tools:** To monitor compliance, organizations need to implement tools that track software and hardware assets, and provide reports on usage and license compliance.

4. **Conduct regular audits:** Regular audits of software and hardware assets can help to identify non-compliance issues and provide opportunities to take corrective action.

5. **Educate employees:** Employee education and training is important for ensuring that employees are aware of their responsibilities related to software and hardware asset management, and for promoting a culture of compliance within the organization.

6. **Develop remediation plans:** In cases where non-compliance issues are identified, organizations need to develop remediation

plans to address the issues and prevent them from recurring.

Achieving ITAM compliance requires a commitment from the organization's leadership, as well as ongoing investment in the necessary tools, processes, and training. However, the benefits of ITAM compliance are significant, including reduced legal and financial risks, improved IT asset management practices, and enhanced overall security and reliability of the IT infrastructure.

## Audit Letter

An audit letter is a formal communication that is sent by an auditor to the management of an organization to confirm the scope and timing of an upcoming audit. The audit letter typically outlines the objectives and procedures of the audit, and may include a request for specific information or documents.

Here are some key components of an audit letter:

1. **Introduction:** The audit letter should include an introduction that explains the purpose of the letter, and the scope and objectives of the upcoming audit.
2. **Audit procedures:** The letter should outline the audit procedures that will be performed, including the areas of the organization that will be audited, the types of documents or

information that will be reviewed, and the timing of the audit.

3. **Requested information:** The letter may include a request for specific information or documents that are necessary for the audit. This may include financial statements, bank statements, and other relevant documents.

4. **Contact information:** The letter should include contact information for the auditor or audit team, including the name, phone number, and email address of the lead auditor.

5. **Deadline:** The letter should include a deadline for responding to the request for information, and for scheduling the audit.

6. **Acknowledgment:** The letter may include a request for the organization to acknowledge receipt of the letter and confirm their agreement with the scope and objectives of the audit.

An audit letter is an important communication that sets the stage for a successful audit. By clearly outlining the objectives and procedures of the audit, and providing a clear request for information or documents, the auditor can help ensure that the audit is conducted efficiently and effectively, and that the organization is fully prepared for the audit process.

Examples of License Data

License data refers to the information that is associated with the software licenses held by an organization. This data can include a wide range of information, such as:

1. **Software vendor:** The name of the vendor or software provider.
2. **Software title:** The name of the software application or product.
3. **License type:** The type of license, such as perpetual, subscription, or concurrent.
4. **License key:** The unique key or code required to activate the software.
5. **License agreement:** The terms and conditions of use for the software, including limitations on use, renewal requirements, and termination clauses.
6. **Number of licenses:** The number of licenses purchased or held by the organization.
7. **Usage metrics:** The metrics used to track the usage of the software, such as the number of installations or users.
8. **License expiration dates:** The date when the license expires, and when it needs to be renewed or replaced.
9. **License costs:** The cost of the license, including any fees, maintenance costs, or support fees.
10. **Compliance status:** Whether the organization is in compliance with the licensing agreement,

or whether there are any compliance issues that need to be addressed.

11. **License owner:** The name of the department or individual that owns the license.

License data is critical for effective software asset management, as it enables organizations to track their software assets, optimize license usage, and ensure compliance with licensing agreements. By maintaining accurate and up-to-date license data, organizations can avoid legal and financial risks, reduce costs, and improve operational efficiency.

## Compliance Enforcement

Compliance enforcement is the process of ensuring that an organization is in compliance with relevant laws, regulations, and policies, and taking corrective action when non-compliance is identified. Compliance enforcement is a critical part of risk management, as non-compliance can lead to legal and financial risks, as well as damage to the organization's reputation.

Here are some key steps for effective compliance enforcement:

1. **Establish clear policies and procedures:** Organizations need to establish clear policies and procedures for compliance with relevant laws, regulations, and policies.
2. **Train employees:** Employees need to be trained on the policies and procedures related

to compliance, and provided with the tools and resources necessary to comply with them.

3. **Monitor compliance:** Regular monitoring of compliance is necessary to identify non-compliance issues and take corrective action. This can include regular audits, assessments, and reviews.

4. **Take corrective action:** When non-compliance issues are identified, organizations need to take corrective action, which may include education and training, changes to policies and procedures, and disciplinary action.

5. **Review and revise policies and procedures:** Policies and procedures related to compliance need to be reviewed and revised on a regular basis to ensure they remain current and effective.

6. **Implement consequences for non-compliance:** Organizations need to establish consequences for non-compliance with policies and procedures, which may include disciplinary action, loss of privileges, or legal action.

Effective compliance enforcement requires a commitment from the organization's leadership, as well as ongoing investment in training, monitoring, and review processes. However, the benefits of effective compliance enforcement are significant, including reduced legal and financial risks, improved operational efficiency, and enhanced reputation and brand value.

Understanding the EULA

A EULA (End User License Agreement) is a legal agreement that outlines the terms and conditions for the use of a software application by an end user. The EULA is a contract between the software vendor and the end user, and it specifies the rights and responsibilities of both parties. Here are some key things to understand about a EULA:

1. **Acceptance:** End users are typically required to accept the terms of the EULA before they can install or use the software. This may be done by clicking a "I agree" button, or by opening the software package or installing the software.

2. **Scope of use:** The EULA defines the scope of use of the software, including the number of installations or users, the devices or platforms on which the software can be used, and any restrictions on use.

3. **Intellectual property:** The EULA specifies the intellectual property rights of the software vendor, including copyrights, trademarks, and patents, and sets out the limitations on the use and distribution of the software.

4. **Warranty and liability:** The EULA outline the warranty and liability provisions for the software, including any disclaimers of warranties and limitations of liability.

5. **Termination:** The EULA specifies the conditions under which the license to use the software

can be terminated, including non-payment of fees, violation of the terms and conditions, or end of the license period.

6. **Updates and upgrades:** The EULA may specify the terms and conditions for updates and upgrades to the software, including whether they are included in the initial purchase or require additional fees.

It is important for end users to carefully read and understand the EULA before agreeing to it. By doing so, end users can ensure that they are aware of the terms and conditions for using the software, and avoid legal and financial risks associated with non-compliance with the EULA.

## Due Diligence for Compliance

Due diligence for compliance refers to the process of taking reasonable steps to ensure that an organization is in compliance with relevant laws, regulations, and policies. Due diligence is an important part of risk management, as it helps to identify and address compliance risks before they become issues.

Here are some key steps for due diligence for compliance:

1. **Identify the relevant laws, regulations, and policies:** The first step is to identify the laws, regulations, and policies that are relevant to the organization's operations. This may include

industry-specific regulations, data privacy laws, environmental regulations, and employment laws.

2. **Assess compliance risks:** Once the relevant laws, regulations, and policies have been identified, the organization needs to assess the compliance risks associated with each of them. This may involve conducting risk assessments, reviewing policies and procedures, and consulting with legal experts.

3. **Develop policies and procedures:** Based on the assessment of compliance risks, the organization needs to develop clear policies and procedures for compliance, which should be communicated to employees and stakeholders.

4. **Train employees:** Employees need to be trained on the policies and procedures related to compliance, and provided with the tools and resources necessary to comply with them.

5. **Monitor compliance:** Regular monitoring of compliance is necessary to identify non-compliance issues and take corrective action. This can include regular audits, assessments, and reviews.

6. **Take corrective action:** When non-compliance issues are identified, organizations need to take corrective action, which may include

education and training, changes to policies and procedures, and disciplinary action.

7. **Review and revise policies and procedures:** Policies and procedures related to compliance need to be reviewed and revised on a regular basis to ensure they remain current and effective.

By taking these steps, organizations can implement an effective due diligence process for compliance, which helps to minimize legal and financial risks, and maintain the organization's reputation and brand value.

The Art of Negotiation

Negotiation is the process of reaching an agreement between two or more parties who have different needs or interests. Negotiation is an essential skill in many areas of life, including business, law, politics, and personal relationships. Here are some key principles to keep in mind when engaging in the art of negotiation:

1. **Preparation:** Effective negotiation requires preparation. This includes gathering information, identifying the other party's needs and interests, and setting clear objectives for what you want to achieve.

2. **Listen actively:** Active listening is an essential component of successful negotiation. By actively listening to the other party, you can gain a deeper understanding of their needs and

interests, and identify opportunities for compromise.

3. **Build rapport:** Building rapport with the other party can help to establish a foundation of trust and respect, which can make it easier to find common ground and reach a mutually beneficial agreement.

4. **Focus on interests, not positions:** Effective negotiation requires focusing on the interests and needs of both parties, rather than on specific positions or demands. This can help to identify opportunities for creative solutions that meet both parties' needs.

5. **Be flexible:** Flexibility is key to successful negotiation. By being willing to consider different options and solutions, you can find common ground and reach a mutually beneficial agreement.

6. **Maintain a positive attitude:** Maintaining a positive and constructive attitude can help to keep the negotiation on track, even in the face of challenges or setbacks.

7. **Be prepared to walk away:** In some cases, it may be necessary to walk away from a negotiation if the other party is not willing to compromise. This can be a difficult decision, but it is important to be prepared to do so if necessary.

Effective negotiation is an art, and requires practice, preparation, and a willingness to listen and find creative solutions. By keeping these principles in mind, negotiators can build successful relationships and reach mutually beneficial agreements with others.

## Ts & Cs Advice

"Ts & Cs" refers to the terms and conditions that govern the use of a product or service, typically laid out in a contract or agreement. Here are some key pieces of advice to keep in mind when dealing with Ts & Cs:

1. **Read and understand the Ts & Cs:** It is important to read and understand the terms and conditions before agreeing to them, as they define the rights and obligations of both parties. If you don't understand a term or provision, ask for clarification or seek legal advice.

2. **Negotiate the Ts & Cs:** Depending on the situation, it may be possible to negotiate the terms and conditions of a contract or agreement. This can include negotiating the scope of the agreement, the payment terms, or the remedies available in case of breach.

3. **Consider the risks:** When reviewing the Ts & Cs, it is important to consider the risks associated with the product or service, as well as the risks associated with the agreement

itself. This may include risks related to data privacy, liability, and intellectual property.

4. **Be aware of hidden costs:** Ts & Cs may include provisions for additional costs or fees that are not immediately apparent. Be sure to read the Ts & Cs carefully to identify any hidden costs or fees that may be associated with the product or service.

5. **Keep a copy of the agreement:** It is important to keep a copy of the agreement, including the Ts & Cs, for future reference. This can be important in case of disputes or questions about the scope or terms of the agreement.

By following these tips, you can navigate the world of Ts & Cs more effectively, and ensure that you are making informed decisions about the products and services you use.

## ITAM Automation

ITAM (Information Technology Asset Management) automation refers to the use of software tools and processes to automate various aspects of IT asset management. By automating ITAM processes, organizations can save time and resources, reduce manual errors, and improve accuracy and efficiency. Here are some key areas where ITAM automation can be beneficial:

1. **Discovery and inventory:** ITAM automation tools can scan an organization's network to

discover and inventory all of its IT assets, including hardware, software, and network devices. This can help organizations to gain a complete and accurate picture of their IT infrastructure.

2. **License management:** ITAM automation tools can help organizations to manage software licenses more effectively by tracking license usage, identifying license overuse, and helping to ensure compliance with licensing agreements.

3. **Contract management:** ITAM automation tools can be used to manage contracts with vendors and service providers, including tracking contract terms, renewal dates, and payment terms.

4. **Risk management:** ITAM automation tools can help organizations to identify and manage risks associated with their IT assets, including security risks, compliance risks, and operational risks.

5. **Reporting and analytics:** ITAM automation tools can provide detailed reporting and analytics on an organization's IT assets, including usage, costs, and performance metrics. This can help organizations to make more informed decisions about their IT investments.

By automating various aspects of ITAM, organizations can streamline their IT asset management processes, reduce costs, and improve the overall efficiency and effectiveness of their IT operations.

## Selecting a Discovery Tool

Selecting the right discovery tool is a critical component of effective IT asset management, as it helps organizations to gain visibility and control over their IT infrastructure. Here are some key factors to consider when selecting a discovery tool:

1.  **Features:** The discovery tool should have the features and functionality that meet the organization's needs. This may include support for different operating systems, the ability to discover and inventory various types of IT assets, and integration with other ITAM tools.
2.  **Scalability:** The discovery tool should be able to handle the size and complexity of the organization's IT infrastructure, and be scalable to support future growth.
3.  **Accuracy:** The discovery tool should be able to provide accurate and up-to-date information on the organization's IT assets, including hardware, software, and network devices.
4.  **Ease of use:** The discovery tool should be easy to use and deploy, with a user-friendly interface that allows IT staff to quickly and easily access and manage the data.

5. **Integration:** The discovery tool should be able to integrate with other ITAM tools, such as license management and contract management software, to provide a complete view of the organization's IT assets.
6. **Vendor support:** The vendor of the discovery tool should have a strong reputation for customer support, with a reliable and responsive support team that can provide assistance when needed.
7. **Cost:** The cost of the discovery tool should be within the organization's budget, and the vendor should provide transparent pricing and licensing options.

By considering these factors when selecting a discovery tool, organizations can find the right tool to meet their ITAM needs, improve their IT asset management processes, and reduce the risks associated with non-compliance and inefficient use of IT assets.

## ITAM Repository

An ITAM (Information Technology Asset Management) repository is a central database or system used to store and manage information about an organization's IT assets, including hardware, software, and network devices. The ITAM repository is an essential component of effective IT asset management, as it provides a single source of truth for all IT asset data, enabling organizations to manage their IT assets more effectively. Here are some key features of an effective ITAM repository:

1. **Comprehensive asset data:** The ITAM repository should contain comprehensive and accurate data on all IT assets, including hardware and software components, licenses, warranties, service agreements, and configurations.
2. **Centralized management:** The ITAM repository should provide a centralized management interface that enables IT staff to access, manage, and update asset data from a single location.
3. **Scalability:** The ITAM repository should be able to handle the size and complexity of the organization's IT infrastructure, and be scalable to support future growth.
4. **Integration:** The ITAM repository should be able to integrate with other ITAM tools, such as discovery and inventory tools, license management software, and contract management systems, to provide a complete view of the organization's IT assets.
5. **Reporting and analytics:** The ITAM repository should provide reporting and analytics tools that enable IT staff to generate reports and dashboards on IT asset data, including usage, costs, and performance metrics.

6. **Security:** The ITAM repository should provide robust security features to ensure that asset data is protected from unauthorized access or modification.
7. **Accessibility:** The ITAM repository should be accessible to all authorized IT staff, regardless of their location or device, to enable collaboration and efficient management of IT assets.

By implementing an effective ITAM repository, organizations can gain greater visibility and control over their IT assets, reduce costs and risks associated with non-compliance and inefficient use of IT assets, and improve the overall efficiency and effectiveness of their IT operations.

## Hardware & Organizational Impacts

IT asset management can have significant hardware and organizational impacts for an organization. Here are some key factors to consider:

1. **Hardware impacts:** Implementing ITAM requires hardware and software tools to collect, process, and manage asset data. This can include inventory and discovery tools, license management software, and other tools. Depending on the size and complexity of the organization's IT infrastructure, these tools can require additional hardware resources, such as

servers or storage devices, which can impact the organization's IT budget and resources.

2. **Organizational impacts:** Implementing ITAM can have significant organizational impacts, as it requires changes to existing processes and workflows, as well as collaboration between different departments and stakeholders. This can include changes to procurement processes, vendor management, and IT support processes. To implement ITAM effectively, organizations may need to establish new roles and responsibilities, such as ITAM program managers, and provide training to staff to ensure they understand their responsibilities.

3. **Standardization:** ITAM can help organizations to standardize their IT assets, which can improve efficiency and reduce costs. By standardizing hardware and software components, organizations can reduce the complexity of their IT infrastructure and improve the reliability and performance of their systems.

4. **Compliance:** ITAM can help organizations to ensure compliance with licensing agreements and regulatory requirements, which can reduce the risk of fines or legal action. By managing software licenses more effectively, organizations can avoid costly over-licensing or

under-licensing, and ensure that they are compliant with licensing agreements.

5. **Cost savings:** Effective ITAM can help organizations to save costs by reducing the costs associated with over-licensing, avoiding hardware and software purchases that are not needed, and extending the life of hardware and software assets. By optimizing the use of IT assets, organizations can maximize the value of their IT investments.

By considering these hardware and organizational impacts, organizations can better plan for the implementation of ITAM, and ensure that they are taking the necessary steps to optimize their IT asset management processes.

## Software Asset Management Glossary

**Software Asset Management (S.A.M):** The set of policies, procedures, and practices used by organizations to manage their software assets throughout their lifecycle, from procurement to disposal.

**License compliance:** Ensuring that an organization's software usage is in compliance with the terms and conditions of the licenses.

**Software inventory:** The process of identifying and cataloging all software assets in an organization's environment.

**Software lifecycle:** The stages that a software asset goes through, from development to disposal.

**Optimization:** The process of maximizing the value of software assets while minimizing their costs.

**Cost reduction:** The process of reducing the overall costs associated with software assets.

**Risk mitigation:** The process of identifying and managing risks associated with software assets.

**Procurement:** The process of acquiring software assets.

**IT:** Information Technology, the department responsible for managing an organization's technology infrastructure and systems.

**Legal:** The department responsible for ensuring an organization's compliance with laws and regulations.

**S.A.M tools:** The software tools used to manage an organization's software assets.

**Cross-functional Collaboration:** The process of bringing together different departments within an organization to work together on S.A.M initiatives.

**Business Alignment:** Ensuring that S.A.M initiatives align with an organization's overall business strategy.

**Software Usage Monitoring:** The process of monitoring and analyzing software usage to identify potential optimization opportunities and risks.

**License Reconciliation:** The process of comparing software licenses with actual usage to ensure compliance and identify potential cost savings.

**Vendor Management:** The process of managing relationships with software vendors.

**Audit Defense:** The process of defending an organization's compliance during a software audit.

**Cloud software management:** The process of managing software assets in a cloud environment.

**Enterprise Agreements:** The agreements between an organization and a software vendor for the purchase and use of software assets.

**Data Analysis:** The process of analyzing data to identify optimization opportunities and risks.

**Asset Disposal:** The process of disposing of software assets that are no longer needed or that are at the end of their life.

**Software Entitlements:** The rights that an organization has to use a software asset.

**Compliance Reporting:** The process of generating reports on an organization's compliance with software licenses and regulations.

**Contract Management:** The process of managing contracts with software vendors.

**License Metrics:** The metrics used to measure software usage for licensing purposes.

**License Terms and Conditions:** The terms and conditions of software licenses that an organization must comply with.

**End-user Training:** The training provided to end-users on how to use software assets.

**Software Renewal Management:** The process of managing the renewal of software licenses.

**Software Catalog:** A catalog of software assets in an organization's environment.

**Self-audit:** The process of auditing an organization's own software usage and compliance.

**License Pooling:** The process of pooling software licenses to maximize their usage.

**Software Metrics:** The metrics used to measure the usage and effectiveness of software assets.

**Governance and Compliance:** The process of ensuring that an organization's software usage is in compliance with legal and regulatory requirements.

**Software Metering:** The process of measuring software usage for licensing and optimization purposes.

**Virtualization:** The process of running multiple virtual machines on a single physical machine.

**Deployment and Installation Management:** The process of deploying and installing software assets in an organization's environment.

**Change Management:** The process of managing changes to software assets in an organization's environment.

**Software as a Service (SaaS) Management:** The process of managing SaaS applications in an organization's environment.

**Bring Your Own Device (BYOD) Policy:** An organization's policy for allowing employees to use their personal devices for work purposes.

**Mobile Device Management (MDM):** The process of managing mobile devices in an organization's environment.

**Information Security:** The process of ensuring the security of an organization's information and data

**Compliance Audit:** The process of auditing an organization's compliance with legal and regulatory requirements.

**Patch Management:** The process of managing software patches to ensure that software assets are up-to-date and secure.

**Open Source License Management:** The process of managing the use of open source software in an organization's environment.

**IT Asset Management (ITAM):** The process of managing an organization's technology assets.

**Maintenance Renewal Management:** The process of managing the renewal of maintenance contracts for software assets.

**Disaster Recovery Planning:** The process of planning for and recovering from disasters that affect an organization's software assets.

**Continuous License Monitoring:** The process of continuously monitoring software usage to ensure compliance and identify potential cost savings.

**Financial Management:** The process of managing the financial aspects of software assets.

**License Negotiations:** The process of negotiating software license terms and conditions with vendors.

**License Optimization:** The process of optimizing software licenses to maximize value and minimize costs.

**Software Analytics:** The process of analyzing software data to identify optimization opportunities and risks.

**Cost Allocation:** The process of allocating software costs to different departments or business units within an organization.

**Procurement Strategy:** An organization's strategy for acquiring software assets.

**Vendor Negotiation:** The process of negotiating with software vendors for the purchase and use of software assets.

**License Transfer:** The process of transferring software licenses from one user or device to another.

**Shadow IT Management:** The process of managing software assets that are used by employees without authorization or oversight.

**ITIL (IT Infrastructure Library) Framework:** A set of best practices for managing IT services and infrastructure.

**ISO 19770 Standard for S.A.M:** The international standard for software asset management.

**Contractual Compliance:** Ensuring compliance with the terms and conditions of software contracts.

**License Types (e.g., perpetual, subscription, concurrent, node-locked):** Different types of software licenses with different terms and conditions.

**License Metrics (e.g., user-based, device-based, server-based, core-based):** The metrics used to measure software usage for licensing purposes.

**Volume Licensing:** A licensing agreement for multiple software assets at a discounted rate.

**License Utilization Analysis:** The analysis of software usage data to identify potential optimization opportunities and risks.

**License Harvesting:** The process of reclaiming unused or underused software licenses.

**License Sharing:** The process of sharing software licenses between users or devices.

**Cloud Service Provider Management:** The process of managing relationships with cloud service providers.

**Asset Tagging:** The process of labeling software assets for tracking and management purposes.

**Proof of Ownership:** The documentation that proves an organization's ownership of software assets.

**Usage Rights:** The rights that an organization has to use software assets.

Software life-cycle Management: The process of managing software assets throughout their lifecycle.

**Centralized Software Management:** The management of software assets from a central location.

**Decentralized Software Management:** The management of software assets from multiple locations.

**User Access Management:** The process of managing user access to software assets.

**Vulnerability Management:** The process of identifying and managing vulnerabilities in software assets.

**Software Piracy Prevention:** The process of preventing unauthorized use of software assets.

**Internal Audit:** The process of auditing an organization's own software usage and compliance.

**External Audit:** The process of auditing an organization's compliance with software licenses and regulations by an external party.

**License Auditing:** The process of auditing an organization's compliance with software licenses.

**Software Deployment Automation:** The process of automating software deployment to reduce errors and increase efficiency.

**Configuration Management:** The process of managing the configuration of software assets.

**Data Privacy Compliance:** The process of ensuring that an organization's software usage is in compliance with data privacy regulations.

www.ingramcontent.com/pod-product-compliance
Lightning Source LLC
LaVergne TN
LVHW051332050326
832903LV00031B/3493

* 9 7 9 8 3 7 7 2 0 4 4 2 8 *